Forecasting Methods
in Sports and Recreation

TO

Malou my wife .... who was "reliable" in her support.

Mylene .... whose best "forecast" is called D.A.A.N.

Marie .... who always reminds me to stay "fit".

Becky .... who does not need a "dummy variable" to explain happiness.

Ariane .... who was quite able to overcome her "multicollinearity" problem (with her sisters).

Forecasting Methods in Sports and Recreation

Antoine Zalatan, Ph.D.

Department of Leisure Studies
University of Ottawa

THOMPSON EDUCATIONAL PUBLISHING, INC.

Toronto

Requests for permission to make copies of any part of the work should be directed to the publisher. Additional copies of this book may be obtained from the publisher.

Orders may be sent to:

Canada
14 Ripley Avenue, Suite 105
Toronto, Ontario
M6S 3N9

United States
240 Portage Road
Lewiston, New York
14092

For faster delivery, please send your order by telephone or fax to:
Tel (416) 766–2763 / Fax (416) 766–0398

Canadian Cataloguing in Publication Data

Main entry under title:

Zalatan, Antoine
Forecasting methods in sports and recreation

Includes bibliographical references and index.
ISBN 1-55077-064-0
1. Recreation - Research - Statistical methods.
2. Sports - Planning - Statistical methods.
3. Recreation - Planning - Statistical methods.
I. Title.

GV14.5.Z35   1994   790'.072   C94-930636-3

Cover design by RHÉAL LEROUX AND ASSOCIATES INC. (OTTAWA).

Printed and bound in Canada.

TABLE OF CONTENTS

LIST OF FIGURES

LIST OF TABLES

ACKNOWLEDGEMENTS

I wish to thank my colleagues from the Leisure Studies Department, University of Ottawa, especially Dr. J.C. Pageot and Dr. D. Dawson who offered helpful suggestions. Appreciation is also extended to my brother Pierre Zalatan (Transport Canada) for his valuable aid. His knowledge of statistics and leisure was a great aid to me. I want to acknowledge the leadership of Dean Henry Edwards of the University of Ottawa who encouraged me in this effort. Erdal Atukeren and Pat Mazepa were more than able research assistants. As well, their diligent reviews highly improved the quality of the final product.

Desirée Zalatan, President of CompuEase Learning Systems (Ottawa) was responsible for many improvements in the manuscript. I am particularly thankful to her. I also wish to express appreciation to the staff of the Office of the Associate Dean of Research, in particular to Ginette Rozon and Francine D'Amour who typed the final version under conditions far from ideal.

PREFACE

The quality of life in all of our communities suffers when there is a lack of resources for leisure services or when such services are poorly planned or administered. Today the need is greater than ever for well-planned, easily available leisure services. For too long a time, park and recreation practitioners and researchers have done an inadequate job of forecasting the leisure behavior patterns of their clients. In most cases, a trial-and-error approach has been used for planning purposes. This is dangerous, often costly, and certainly inefficient. Antoine Zalatan's book *Forecasting Methods in Sports and Recreation* is a welcome addition to the literature and will assist greatly in reducing many of these problems.

The author does an excellent job of explaining in a very practical way the various qualitative forecasting methods as well as market forecasting methods of forecasting. Excellent examples are given that assist the reader in following the procedures.

Most importantly, Dr. Zalatan explains the importance of forecasting and the need for preciseness. The book evaluates each of the forecasting methods and their application in a way that helps the user select the most appropriate method for their purpose.

The information derived from the use of these models will help park and recreation administrators in their decision-making process regarding questions on future facilities and personnel and how business entrepreneurs will identify markets for leisure and recreation programs before they make significant investments. It will assist resource managers on the best mix of access, sites, and amenities. The models suggested in this book will eliminate many of the myths and beliefs we have taken for granted.

Dr. Zalatan's book discusses in detail four important questions: What is the purpose of forecasting? What are the components of the recreation system for which the forecast will be made? How important is the past in estimating the future? Which forecasting technique should be used?

This book bridges a serious gap by providing a basic process through which park and recreation personnel can learn specific knowledge and functional skills about forecasting techniques. It links scientific knowledge with actual examples of situations that administrators and planners encounter as they look to the future.

Students, administrators, and educators will find this volume an excellent resource, one that will hone their skills as planners and decision makers. The book also affords greater insight into the nature of sport and recreation operation and the myriad of situations that recreation professionals encounter in their provision of opportunities for meaningful leisure expression.

Joseph J. Bannon, Ph.D.
Professor Emeritus
University of Illinois
1994

1

FORECASTING ENVIRONMENT

"The Future isn't what it used to be".

W.C. Fields

1.1 INTRODUCTION

"Must this torture be tormenting when it bring us greater law?"

Insel

When Joseph made an interpretation of the Pharaoh's dream, he delivered the first forecast of "agriculture cycles" or "business cycles": seven fat cows and seven lean cows, which are symbolic of prosperity and recession years. This biblical image is unfair to modern forecasting methods, which are no longer a sort of intuition exercise, an act of prophecy, or a result of wild imagination. We have no firm knowledge of the forecasting methods that were used by the ancient world, but we do know at least, that forecasting needs existed, and that Joseph was rewarded for his performance. The lesson from this biblical story is that forecasts serve an important purpose and are an essential prerequisite of planning and efficient action. Even if they are difficult, imprecise and sometimes proven wrong, we are left with two choices: "do it" or, like the traveller to Dante's "Inferno", abandon all hope. We simply cannot throw up our hands and say "no more forecasting". This is a counsel of despair that leads nowhere.

In today's world, the complexity of our socio-economic systems, the multiplicity of choices and the increasing uncertainty underscore the need to forecast, applying scientific methods. Crystal balls have been replaced by calculators, computers and methods essentially based on sound foundations, tested and verified by previous experiences. This book discusses and evaluates these methods and their applications in such a way as to allow practitioners to compare, choose and utilize the method most suited to their purpose.

In the area of sports and recreation, the strong demand for facilities is creating striking opportunities for future developments and, at the same time, formidable problems of forecasting. Bad decisions could clearly lead to resources being wasted on a very large scale and could cause serious distortions in the development of public and private supply. For example, an underestimation of future demand could result in a shortage of facilities. This is particularly important under conditions of increasing demand. Indeed,

- there is a need to reduce uncertainty;
- unanticipated changes may develop quickly;
- fast growth in certain areas cannot continue forever;
- unexpected events do occur; and
- interdependence between components of the system is a fact of life.

Managers of services, facilities and programs must be able to estimate, with a time lead, the expected level of future demand and resources needed to be allocated, and the facilities to be organized accordingly. Used in this way, forecasting becomes a planning tool and cannot be omitted from serious planning. It provides, essentially, the required information to aid planners who are charged with the task of evaluating the need for new facilities. Reliable forecasting of future demand is an important requirement for regional, provincial, state and national policies regarding provision of sports and recreation opportunities. The private sector is also continually introducing new facilities and expanding existing ones. Forecasts are required in all situations in which a current choice or decision has future implications. Good decision-making can become better or worse, depending on the quality of the forecasts that underlie the decision-making process. In general, lack of knowledge and the growing uncertainty affecting our environment dictate a strong need for forecasting. This is illustrated by the following:

1) The public and private *planning and budgetary allocation* process requires knowledge of future demand in order to allocate resources efficiently. Forecasting consumption is important in terms of planning investments in facilities and identifying new markets and products.

2) Estimation of demand for planning purposes is also highly connected to *benefits evaluation*. The evaluation and measurement of benefits necessitate demand forecasts. In turn, benefit evaluation can be used in cost/benefit models, as a guide to resource

allocation in the public sector and as a benchmark in investment decisions in the private sector.

3)   The *issue of cost recovery* is raised more and more often in the context of financing sports and recreation. For instance, in the area of outdoor recreation, recent studies show that most users accept fees as a reasonable method of paying for outdoor recreation activities. An analysis of future demand can identify the pressures on the existing supply of facilities and assist in determining the marginal cost of serving this additional demand, whether by direct financing or on a pay-as-you-go basis.

4)   It is often suggested that sports and recreation events have a beneficial *impact on the regional economy.* Despite the differences in the methods used to calculate the regional economic impact, it is safe to conclude that any evaluation of site-demand forecasts would certainly aid in local planning and the assessment of economic benefits.

5)   An assessment of future demand can certainly assist in the overall measurement of the *derived demand for the inputs* required to produce sports and recreation opportunities, including capital and natural resources as well as trained personnel.

6)   In constructing forecasting models, our knowledge of the determinants of demand is enhanced, and usually a serious effort is made to evaluate the possible levels of these explanatory variables in the future. Thus, forecasting becomes more than a "game of numbers". It is a dynamic process that identifies and analyzes the causal *relationship between demand and the socio-economic structures* that impact upon it.

The leisure and sports world of the 1960s and earlier was more stable than now. The number of activities was limited, infrastructures and operating budgets were modest and volunteers were the dominant organizing personnel. The situation today is different. Sport is now quite an elaborate industry, and leisure covers a wide array of dimensions, from outdoor parks to health clubs and electronic arcades. This change and instability are exerting pressures on the professional to ensure that his/her knowledge of the future is adequate. As a consequence, interest and investment in forecasting methods have been growing and the need to train professionals in the "forecasting art" is becoming a necessity.

This book does not attempt to turn leisure and sports experts into complete forecasting experts. Forecasting is a tricky business and, even if one masters the techniques, experience and sound judgement are essential. Indeed, one of the most fundamental problems we are facing is the imbalance between advances in technology and our capacity to anticipate and adjust to the social changes needed to accommodate such technological change. This imbalance will increase uncertainty about the future and will give to forecasting activity, using judgements and techniques, a major role in identifying the social changes needed for homeostasis and avoiding social disaster.

1.2 WHY FORECASTING?

"The future usually arrives before we are ready".

Anonymous

A day can hardly pass by without situations arising where decisions have to be reached. Some of these decisions are fairly simple and do not require complex evaluations or in-depth analysis of future implications:

- *Will I buy a bow-tie or a bottle of Montrachet wine?*
- *Should I attend Les Misérables or the Phantom of The Opera?*

In other situations, decisions are uncertain and complex, and necessitate a thorough knowledge of the determining factors:

- *What is the best way to invest the two million dollars I won in the lottery?*
- *As director of a community centre, do I expect the number of participants to increase next year? What will be the size of the demand and why?*
- *Given the composition of the National Hockey League this season, what revenues can be expected from entrance fees?*
- *Taking into consideration the size of the publicity budget of this year, how many non-resident visitors should the "Winterlude" festival's organizers expect?*

Such decisions can be reached with or without the use of structured forecasting methods. The ultimate efficiency in the decisions rests on our capacity to forecast accurately, particularly when the situation is complex and the choice and outcome not evident. Indeed, forecasting is possible and desirable only when the following two conditions are met:

1) *The decision to be attained is not unique and a choice does exist.* The absence of choice clearly determines the action to be taken. Forecasting is redundant when only a unique option is available. It is like the story of a King being greeted by a governor who apologized for not being able to honour him with the traditional twenty-one gun salute. The governor informed the King that ten reasons prevented him from fulfilling his obligation: "The first reason, your majesty, is the lack of gun powder". Obviously, the nine other reasons were unimportant. The decision is clear when one is confronted with a unique choice.

2) *The outcome of the decision is uncertain.* The benefits attached to a forecasting exercise usually increase with the complexity of the expected results and decrease with the probability of their occurrence. Certainty eliminates the need to forecast. For instance, if the budget of a sportsplex centre is fixed for the next three years, it would be absurd to establish a financial forecast. Or if the local arena is totally booked for the next two years it is useless to apply forecasting methods to determine amount of use.

1.3 PREPARATORY GROUNDS

"Hilde: Ah, master builder! My beautiful, beautiful castle! Our castle in the Air!
Solness: Built on a firm foundation!"

Henrik Ibsen, *The Master Builder*

Successful forecasting begins by answering the following questions:

What is the purpose of the forecast?

The answer to this question will determine the accuracy, power and selection of the forecasting techniques. The level of inaccuracy that can be tolerated should be fixed. This allows the forecaster to trade off cost against accuracy in choosing a technique. For instance, if we have to forecast the shortage in municipal recreational land over the next five years and recommend some changes in land reallocation and rezoning, a forecasting error of 10 percent may be too high. On the other hand, if the purpose of the forecast is to predict the future salaries of baseball players, a deviation of 10 percent is likely to be acceptable.

What are the components of the recreation system for which the forecast will be made?

This question requests clarification of the relationships of interacting variables. For instance, if a recreation site offers ground as well as water activities, it is essential to determine participation in both segments in order to properly forecast the orientation of future demand. Once the variables and their relationships are clarified, the forecaster can build a causal model of the system that captures both the facts and the logic of the situation.

Moreover, the question should be raised as to what constitutes a "recreation system". Should attendance at state parks, historic sites and wildlife areas be forecasted using the same model? Or should a separate method be applied for each of these groups?

How important is the past in estimating the future?

It is essential to identify recent changes that, in addition to having an impact on present demand, may exert a greater impact in the future. Significant changes in the demand diminish the similarity of past and future. Over the short term, recent changes are unlikely to cause overall patterns to alter, but over the long term their effects are likely to increase. The environment awareness and its effect on sports and recreation is indicative of new developments that should be considered in future forecasts. Unfortunately, it is seldom possible to incorporate the impact of these "disturbances" in a forecasting model, due to a lack of quantification or to the limited information at hand. It is at this level that human judgement is applied and the effect of the exogenous variables evaluated. Often this is done by using "optimistic" or "pessimistic" values for the forecasted variables, or adjusting the forecast by a certain factor presumably accounting for the disturbance.

Which forecasting technique should be used?

To handle the increasing variety and complexity of forecasting problems, many techniques have been developed. Each has its special use, and care must be taken to select the correct technique for a particular application. The selection of a method depends on several factors, including:

- *The environment of the forecast;*
- *Availability of data;*
- *Degree of accuracy aimed at;*
- *The time period;*

.   *The cost/benefit or value of the forecast; and/or*

.   *The lead time available for developing the forecast.*

In general, the forecaster should choose a technique that makes the best use of available data. For instance, if a series of demands is characterized by strong seasonal variations, it is ill-advised to use trend projections. A recursive model or the "exponential smoothing technique" will obviously yield better results. If one can readily apply one technique of acceptable accuracy, one should not try to "gold-plate" it by using a more advanced technique that offers potentially greater accuracy but requires information that is costly to obtain or non-existent.

In general, the selection of a forecasting method must be based on an economic criterion; the cost of producing the forecast must be weighted against the benefits obtained. However, these benefits are often difficult to estimate a priori and can best be evaluated only after the forecast has been applied. Hence, the choice among forecasting methods must be made regardless of the expected results.

A forecaster should ask the following questions before any statistical analyses begin:

.   *What is the purpose of the forecast?*

.   *What decisions will be based on the forecast?*

.   *How will the forecast be used?*

.   *Who are the main users of the forecast?*

.   *Given the level of knowledge of the user, what is the best form in which to present a forecast?*

.   *Which variables affect the variable being forecasted?*

.   *What data is needed?*

.   *Is the needed data available?*

1.4 STUDY QUESTIONS

1) Why is it important to establish reliable forecasting of future demand for sports and recreation activities? Provide examples to support your arguments.

→ efficent decisions

2) Can you establish a relationship between forecasting levels of demand and user's fees? Explain.

3) Identify areas of sports and recreation (activities and facilities) where forecasting is highly needed.

4) Why is the past important in determining the future?

5) "All decision-makers want to know what was going to happen in the future and what the effects of their own decisions would be, so that they could evaluate the consequences of any alternative courses of action". Is the above sentence valid in the area of sports and recreation? Provide examples to support your answer.

6) "Forecasting is possible and desirable only when two conditions are met": name these two conditions and give a brief explanation of both.

7) What four preparatory questions should be asked when planning to forecast future demand of, for example, a new multi-use indoor sport facility?

8) Name eight questions a forecaster should ask before any statistical analyses begin.

9) How important is accuracy in forecasting?

10) Name several factors which should be considered when selecting a forecasting technique.

11) Which specific economic criterion should be considered in selecting a forecasting method?

12) How can forecasting be used to indicate the benefits of, for example, a new hockey arena, or indoor swimming pool?

13) How would an evaluation of site-demand forecasts aid in assessment of the economic benefits of a sporting or recreational event?

1.5 BIBLIOGRAPHY

ALBERT, S.
1974 *Political Science and the Study of the Future*, Hinsdale IL: Dryden Press.

ARMSTRONG, J.S.
1989 Combining Forecasts: The End of the Beginning or the Beginning of the End?, *International Journal of Forecasting* 5, 4, 585-588.

ARMSTRONG, J.S.
1978 *Long-Range Forecasting: From Crystal Ball to Computer*, New York, NY: John Wiley and Sons.

BANGAY, J. (ed.)
1984 *Aquatic Programming: Reaching Today's Market, Proceedings of the 1983 Symposium, Ottawa, Ontario*, Toronto, ON: Royal Life Saving Society Canada.

BANGAY, J. (ed.)
1980 *National Outdoor Recreation Trend Symposium Broomal, PA.*, Durham, NH: National Outdoor Recreation Trends Symposium.

BANGAY, J. (ed.)
1978 *Proceedings - Canadian Congress on Leisure Research*, Laval, PQ: Presses de l'Université Laval.

BECKER, H.S.
1985 "Making Futures Research Useful: The Practitioner's Opportunity", *Futures Research Quarterly*, Vol. 1, 15-28.

BELL, W.
1987 "Is the Futures Field an Art Form or Can it Become a Science?", *Futures Research Quarterly*, Vol. 3, 27-44.

BURTON, T.L.
1981 You Can't Get There from Here: A Perspective on Recreation Forecasting in Canada, *Recreation Research Review*, 9, 38-43.

BUTTS, F.B.
1985 Corporate Recreation and Fitness: Direction and Future, *Texas Association HPERD Journal*, 54 (1), 16, 51.

CARRE, F.A. (ed.)
1988 *I.C.P.E.R./C.A.H.P.E.R. World Conference Towards the 21st Century*, Vancouver, BC: University of British Columbia.

CHAMBERS, J.C., S.K. MULLICK and D.D. SMITH
1974 *An Executive's Guide to Forecasting*, New York, NY: John Wiley and Sons.

CHAMBERS, J.C., S.K. MULLICK, and D.D. SMITH
1971 "How to Choose the Right Forecasting Technique", *Harvard Business Review*, Vol. 49, 71-72.

CHELLADURAI, P.
1991 Management, In *The Management of Sport: Its Foundations and Application*, St. Louis, MO: Moresby-Year Book Inc.

CICCHETTI, C.
1973 *Forecasting Recreation in the United States*, Lexington, Mass: D.C. Heath and Co.

CLEMENT, A.
1990 The Future of Sport and Fitness, In Parks, J.B. and Zanger, B.R.K. (eds.), *Sport and Fitness Management: Career Strategies and Professional Content*, Champaign, IL: Human Kinetics Books, 257-265.

CORNISH, E.
1977 *The Study of the Future: An Introduction to the Art and Science of Understanding and Shaping Tomorrow's World*, Washington: The Society.

DAUB, M.
1984 "Some Reflections on the Importance of Forecasting to Policy Making", *Canadian Public Policy*, Vol. 10 (4), 377-383.

DOHERTY, S.
1993 Tracking the Trends and Facing the Future, *Active Living*, 2 (2), 3; 6.

DUFFIELD, B.S.
1976 Forecasting Leisure Futures: An Exercise in Understanding and Analysis, In Howarth, J.T. and S.R. Parker (eds.) *Forecasting Leisure Futures*, London: Leisure Studies Assoc. 33-48.

ENCEL, S. and P.K. MARSTRAND and W. PAGE
1975 *The Art of Anticipation: Values and Methods in Forecasting*, London: Martin Robertson.

GIRGINOV, V.
1989 Leisure and Leisure Sports in East Europe Countries: Predictions for the Year 2000,

Journal of the International Council for Health, Physical Education and Recreation, 26 (1), 4-7.

GREENDORFER, S.L.
1989   Catch the Vision. Future Directions for Women in Sport, *Journal of Physical Education, Recreation and Dance*, 60 (3), 31-32.

HEINEMANN, K.
1986   The Future of Sports: Challenge for the Science of Sport, *International Review for the Sociology of Sport*, 21 (4), 271-285.

HELMER, O. and N. RESCHER
1964   *Report of a Long-Range Forecasting Study*, Paper p-2982, Santa Monica, CA: Rand Corporation.

HELMER, O. and N. RESCHER
1960   *On the Epistemology of the Exact Sciences*, Paper R-353, Santa Monica, CA: Rand Corporation.

HOF, J.G.
1980   Problems in Projecting Recreation Resource Use Through Supply and Demand Analysis, In Hawkins, Shafer, and Rovelstad, (eds.) *Tourism Planning and Development Issues*, Washington, DC: George Washington University, 443-461.

HORNA, J.L.A.
1989   Trends in Sports in Canada, In Kamphorts, T.J. and Roberts, K. (eds.), *Trends in Sports: A Multinational Perspective*, Culemborg, Netherlands: Giordano Bruno, 33-65.

HOWORTH, J.T. and S.R. PARKER (eds.)
1976   *Forecasting Leisure Futures*, London: Leisure Studies Assoc.

INTERNATIONAL COMMITTEE FOR SOCIOLOGY OF SPORT
1987   *Physical Culture and Sports in the Way of Life of the Young Generation*, Prague: International Committee for Sociology of Sport.

JOHNSTON, W.E.
1981   Predicting Future Outdoor Recreation Demand and Uses, *Outdoor Recreation and the Public Interest*, Proceedings of the 1979 Meeting of W-133, R.L. Gum and L.M. Arthur (eds.) Special Report No. 610, Corvallis: Oregon State University.

KAMPHORTS, T.J. and K. ROBERTS
1989   *Trends in Sports: A Multinational Perspective*, Culemborg, Netherlands: Giordano Bruno.

KARLQVIST
1991   *Beyond Belief: Randomness Prediction and Explanation in Science*, Boca Raton, Fla: CRC Press.

KELLY, J.R.
1989   "Trends in Sports in the United States of America", In Kamphorts, T.J. and Roberts, K. (eds.), *Trends in Sports: A Multinational Perspective*, Culemborg, Netherlands: Giordano Bruno, 67-89.

KENNEY, M.L.
1988   "Planning the Future: A Voyage of Discovery", *Futures Research Quarterly*, Vol. 4, 49-74.

LIEBER, S.R. and D.R. FESENMAIER (eds.)
1983   *Recreation Planning and Management*, State College, PA: Venture Publishing Inc.

LONSDALE, R.C.
1975   "Futures Research, Policy Research, and the Policy Sciences", *Education and Urban Society*, Vol. 7 (3), 246-293.

LOYE, D.
1978   *The Knowable Future: A Psychology of Forecasting and Prophecy*, New York, NY: Wiley.

MAGUIRE, M. and D.R. YOUNGER
1978   HCRS Sheds Light on Recreation Trends with Future Forecasting, *Parks and Recreation*, 15 (5), 60-61: 63-66.

MASSENGALE, J.E. (ed.)
1987   *Trends Toward the Future in Physical Education*, Champaign, IL: Human Kinetics Publishers, Inc.

PARKS, J.B. and B.R.K. ZANGER (eds.)
1990   *Sport and Fitness Management: Career Strategies and Professional Content*, Champaign, IL: Human Kinetics Books.

PARKHOUSE, B.L. (ed.)
1991   *The Management of Sport: Its Foundations and Application*, St. Louis, MO: Moresby-Year Book Inc.

RESCHER, N.
1967 *The Future as an Object of Research*, Paper P-3593, Santa Monica, CA: Rand Corporation.

RICHARDSON, J.M. Jr.
1987 "Global Modelling: A Retrospective", *Futures Research Quarterly*, Vol. 3, 5-26.

ROMER, K.G.
1986 *Corporate Health Promotion and the Post-Industrial Society: a Futures Study in Health Forecasting*, Eugene, OR: Microform Publications.

SAATY, T.L.
1990 *Embracing the Future: Meeting the Challenge of Our Changing World*, New York, NY: Praeger.

SHAFER, E.L. Jr. and G.H. MOELLER
1974 Through the Looking Glass in Environmental Management, *Parks and Recreation* 9, 20-23; 48; 49.

SHEFFIELD, E.A. and K. DAVIS
1986 The Academician's Role in the Theoretical Development of Sport Management, *Physical Educator*, 43 (4), 183-187.

SHERRILL, C.
1983 The Future is Ours to Shape, *Physical Educator*, 40 (1), 44-50.

SULLIVAN, W.G. and W.W. CLAYCOMBE
1977 *Fundamentals of Forecasting*, Reston, VA: Reston Publishing Company.

VEAL, A.J. (note - has Chap on the Lsr forecasting tradition)
1987 *Leisure and the Future*, London: Allen & Unwin Pub. Ltd.

VEAL, A.L.
1987 The Leisure Forecasting Tradition, Ch 7 of *Leisure and the Future*, London: Allen & Unwin, 125-156.

VICKERMAN, R.W.
1983 The Contribution of Economics to the Study of Leisure: A Review, *Leisure Studies (London)*, 2 (3), 345-364.

WAGAR, W.W.
1986 "Profile of a Futurist: Arnold J. Toynbee and the Coming World of Civilization", *Futures Research Quarterly*, Vol. 2, 61-71.

WETZEL, J.N.
1977   Estimating Benefits of Recreation Under Conditions of Congestion, *Journal of Environmental Economics and Management*, 4 (3), 239-246.

WILKINSON, G.F.
1988   "Why did you use that Forecasting Technique?", *The Journal of Business Forecasting*, Fall, 2-4.

ZEIGLER, E.F.
1988   Looking to the Future in Physical Education and Sport (with Implications for the International Arena), In Carre, F.A. (ed.), *I.C.P.E.R./C.A.H.P.E.R. World Conference Towards the 21st Century*, Vancouver, BC: University of British Columbia.

ZEIGLER, E.F.
1977   Future as History in Sport and Physical Education, *Canadian Journal of Applied Sport Sciences*, 2 (1), 1-8.

ZUZANEK, J.
1978   Leisure Trends and Social Forecasting (Thirteen Propositions), In *Proceedings - Canadian Congress on Leisure Research* Laval, PQ: Presses de l'Université Laval, 156-160.

_____

1990   Planning the Future, *Sports Information Bulletin (Brussels)* 23, 1643-1666.

Qualitative (vs) Quantitative.

2

QUALITATIVE FORECASTING METHODS

"Some people have given the impression that there is a conflict between model forecasts and subjective forecasts: not at all! Subjective forecasts are based on judgement - judgement is important and since people with good judgement are not numerous, they should be valued highly!"

Gwilym M. Jenkins

2.1 NEED

"If you talk about the future, even the demons will laugh".

Japanese Saying

A forecasting method is called "qualitative" or "judgemental" when the forecasting procedure used cannot be described well enough to let another forecaster use it and arrive at the same result. Common opinion might suggest that qualitative methods are the best methods, and stories abound of cases where management made amazing forecasts simply on the basis of a "hunch", "judgement", or "instinct". However, we tend to remember only the accurate forecasts and forget the "fiasco cases". This does not mean that qualitative methods do not have a *raison d'être*. The qualitative method offers an advantage when the forecaster's choice is limited due to a lack of adequate data (e.g. no records, new area or product, data recorded is inadequate...) or when the factors affecting the forecast may be better handled qualitatively. For example:

- predicting major socio-economic changes that, in turn, can affect leisure;
- forecasting new types of camping;
- predicting the introduction of new electronic games;
- forecasting the impact of new environmental regulations on certain outdoor activities; and
- projecting the effect of a reduction in the workweek.

In some situations the "qualitative" and the "quantitative" techniques may complement each other. For instance, qualitative techniques might predict areas where health clubs would develop a profitable market, whereas quantitative methods would try to forecast the actual levels of profits, turning points and new directions.

In general, qualitative methods of forecasting are applicable in situations where numerical data do not exist, or for very long-term forecasts where the underlying relationships of a time series are likely to change substantially. Qualitative forecasts rely largely on human judgement, although some input of a quantitative nature may complement the qualitative technique. In fact, better forecasts may be arrived at by combining a model (quantitative) and a judgemental (qualitative) forecast. The choice is not necessarily determined by the level of expertise or the forecasting budget, but rather by the nature of the problem at hand.

2.2 LOGICAL ESTIMATES METHOD

"Well, I shan't go, at any rate, said Alice; besides, that's not a regular rule: you invented it just now. It's the oldest rule in the book, said the King. Then it ought to be Number One, said Alice."

Lewis Carroll, *Alice in Wonderland*

2.2.1 STEPS

Making estimates or "educated guesses" is often a useful method of forecasting. It may be used when:

- there is no other way of predicting something (a new product or services);
- the range of possible alternatives and the accuracy requirements are such that a more complex study is not justified; or
- the results are not very sensitive to the estimated factor within the range of estimate.

In most cases, estimates have to be used for non-quantifiable variables. The simpler the activity or characteristic, the easier it is to make a realistic estimate for it. Therefore, the reliability of estimates can be greatly improved by breaking down the problem into its components. Examples of an a "educated guess" forecast may include:

- a theatre group forecasting ticket sales for their new play;

- a sports goods store predicting monthly sales of a new brand of sport shoes to ensure adequate inventory stock; or

- the manager of a sportsplex, forecasting attendance at the year-end "sports tournament".

2.2.2 EVALUATION

This approach to forecasting does not follow any specific method. It is solely based on the knowledge and the experience of the forecaster and, consequently, similar situations may lead and produce different results. Using "educated guesses" is advisable only when forecasting errors do not have a strong influence on the problem at hand. The main advantage of the method is that it draws directly on the knowledge of the individuals directly concerned with the problem at hand.

2.3 NOMINAL GROUP METHOD

"A committee is twelve men doing the work of one".

Arthur Block, <u>Murphy's Law</u>

2.3.1 STEPS

This process involves bringing together experts who are knowledgeable in the area of interest. These individuals act as a group in name only; they are assembled in a rigorously structured meeting where direct communication is excluded. The members of the group suggest ideas (i.e., forecast) and then vote as to the selection of the ideas. The forecast receiving the highest score is generally the one adopted.

Steps involved in this method are:

1) Selection of the group of individuals knowledgeable in the area under discussion (7-10 members). Upon arriving in the room, the individuals are seated around a table and asked not to communicate with one another.

2) They are then instructed to write down their ideas concerning the topic. Once ideas have been jotted down, a secretary is designated to record the ideas as they are presented, for all to see.

3) The individuals take turns presenting their ideas one at a time, until every one has contributed an idea and/or has no more ideas left.

4)   Each of the ideas is then discussed in a structured format. The hope here is to clarify the idea to everyone, allowing a more enlightened decision to be made. It is important to allot each idea roughly the same amount of discussion time.

5)   Each member of the group then prioritizes the ideas and votes by secret ballot.

6)   With the totals of each idea tabulated, the forecaster generally adopts the idea (i.e. forecast) receiving the most points.

2.3.2 EVALUATION

The structured format of the method and the adoption of the highest score convey the image of a "quantitative method" and precision. In fact this is not the case, and effort to reduce communication among the experts limits the generation of ideas.

2.4 EXPERT METHOD

"... a lawyer who has not studied economics and sociology is very apt to become a public enemy".

L.D. Brandeis

An expert is anyone who has special skills in, or knowledge of, a particular subject. The expert may be part of the organization or simply hired as a consultant. He identifies the problem, studies whatever material he can find on the subject and then prepares his best estimate about the future. Experts often make individual forecasts from which a consensus is reached through discussion.

2.4.1 STEPS

Forecasts can be obtained from experts in three forms:

1) **Point forecasts**

This is a forecast of a specific level. It provides the least amount of information, and serves its purpose from the management viewpoint. Point forecasts can take the following form:

> *"Next year the number of participants at the Long Run Marathon is expected to reach the 1,000 level".*

Point forecasts are the simplest forecast to make, because they give the least information. They are almost certain to be wrong, but there is no indication of how much or with what probability. For this reason, it is desirable to obtain forecasts in either an interval or a probability-distribution form.

2) **Interval forecasts** ─Dwithina range,

This is a forecast that falls within a stated range and within a given level of confidence. Thus, the forecaster will usually provide "higher" and "lower" forecasts, and assign to each a certain level of confidence. Interval forecasts can take the following form:

> *"Next year the number of participants at the Long Run Marathon is expected to be in the 900 to 1,200 range".*

3)   Probability forecasts

This is a forecast where two or more possibilities are assigned to two or more possible intervals.   Thus, a forecaster using this approach would forecast the number of participants for the Long Run Marathon in the following form:

Number of participants	Probability of occurrence
600	0.20
900	0.30
1,100	0.50

From the above numbers and the associated probability of occurrence, a "point forecast" can be obtained as follows:

Number of of participants		Probability		Total
600	x	0.20	=	120
900	x	0.30	=	270
1,100	x	0.50	=	550
Point forecast				*940*

Expert opinion is usually required for making forecasts in situations where:

- *the area of work is poorly structured;*
- *progress or change is more dependent on external socio-economic factors;*
- *political, ethical or moral considerations play an important role;*
- *historical data are lacking; or*
- *the product or event is reasonably new.*

2.4.2 EVALUATION

At the outset, it should be noted that the quality of such forecasts is influenced by many variables, including the following points:

. *The level of expertise of the forecaster.* While objective criteria such as years of experience and level of education can be applied to define "expertise", the problem becomes more difficult to handle when forecasting deals with a non-homogenous product or service. An expert in aquatic products may have a lesser aptitude to forecast participation or sales of golf equipment.

. *Influence of other forecasters.* If "peer-pressures" or "hierarchial power" are present, this influence may induce the forecaster to modify his forecast. While these interactions may be viewed in a positive way, they interfere with the initial forecast and may create a convergence to the most dominant forecaster, who is not necessarily the most accurate one.

. *Resources constraints.* Often the forecaster is allowed minimum resources (time and materials) to produce his forecast. Management may take the following for granted: if he is the "expert" then he should be capable of producing a forecast with minimum resources and time. His expertise stands as the best guarantee for an expedient and (hopefully) accurate forecast.

While the method is simple and "experts" are usually readily available in the government and in the private sector, this method has several weaknesses, mainly:

. The forecasts are often so vague that it is difficult to determine whether a forecast has been either accurate or inaccurate.

. The forecasts include few or no explicit reasons for the forecasted level.

. No real methodology is followed. If the forecast turns out to be correct, it is impossible for others to use the same method, and if it is incorrect the methodology cannot be modified in order to improve the accuracy level.

2.5 AGGREGATION METHOD

"We are not amused".

Queen Victoria

2.5.1 STEPS

This method is often used by the manufacturers of sporting products and equipment. Market representatives are usually asked to make estimates of their sales by product for each customer and for potential customers for the forecast period. These results are then aggregated to obtain an overall sales forecast. The rationale supporting this technique is supported by the following arguments:

. Each salesperson is more knowledgeable about his or her own area of revenue-generation.

. Aggregation minimizes potential forecasting errors. If a particular forecast appears "out of line", the impact on the aggregated forecast may be minimal and this particular forecast may be reviewed, corrected or rejected.

. This forecasting approach lends a sense of responsibility to field representatives. Forecasting and planning decisions become an integral part of their regular duties, and they are encouraged to contribute to the overall control function of the firm.

.   Estimates obtained by regional managers may be revised due to their "upward" or "downward" bias. This revision may be based on the judgement of senior management, and on previous forecasts and experience.

In the areas of sports and recreation, the "Aggregation Method" can be applied to situations such as:

-    forecasting total park attendancc by aggregating data obtained from each park manager;

-    forecasting total enrolment in sport leagues by aggregating individual enrolment at different arenas, clubs, or regions; or

-    forecasting participation in municipal recreation by adding up the main segments of the program.

2.5.2 EVALUATION

Despite its simplicity and the operational appeal of being directly derived from the field where the action is, the technique presents a few problems, namely:

.   The field persons might not possess the necessary knowledge or skill to prepare an accurate forecast.

.   There is a tendency to produce "optimistic" forecasts if times are good and "pessimistic" forecasts if times are hard. Worse, if times are hard there is often an uncritical assumption that things must soon improve.

.   It is usually accepted that being at the root of the operational level may be a disadvantage in forecasting. People tend to over-react to good or bad situations, and forecasts therefore tend to display an "optimistic" or "pessimistic" bias.

- Operational level individuals have more skills in "day-to-day" management than in forecasting.

- There is a general tendency among "untrained personnel" to associate forecasting with higher levels of activities. Projecting into the future implies higher levels of activities, and an upward bias may then crop into the forecast.

- Regional or unit managers usually correlate a "higher" forecast with "higher" budgets. Thus the tendency to produce more optimistic forecasts would have a positive effect on their operational budgets.

- Regional staff would often consider the exercise as just another requirement to increase "paperwork".

- While operational people are usually quite aware of, and sensitive to changes at their "micro-level", they are often unaware of broad economic movements or trends and their likely effects on their activity forecast.

If the method has to be used, the following steps would help improve its accuracy:

- supply each field forecaster with his past work record as well as his past forecasting performance;

- provide a "general forecast" on the business and industry outlook as well as regional economic forecasts, if applicable;

- grant pay or monetary rewards for the accuracy of the forecasting performance;

- do not limit the forecast to a "number-generation exercise"; explanatory notes should accompany each forecast; and discuss each forecast and provide ample opportunities for the forecaster to exchange views and analyze the results.

Aggregation Method Option (handwritten)

In general, this method is reasonably accurate in the very short term (1 to 6 months) and fair to-good in the short term (6 months to a year), but poor over periods that exceed one year.

2.6 PANEL CONSENSUS

"Mein Herr Marquis, ein Mann wie Sie Sollt besser das verstehn".
My dear Marquis, a man like you ought to know better than that.

Johann Strauss Jr.

2.6.1 STEPS

This method is very similar to the "Expert Method" in its application. However, the composition of the panel is different; it reflects the operational interdependence of individuals rather than their level or area of expertise. For instance, the "socio-economic branch" of a government department or the "Sports and Recreation Supervisors" of a municipal administration might get together to seek the opinion of their staff and forecast future levels of operations. The panel is usually comprised of individuals related to the following groups:

- panel of experts who are not associated with the operations of the company or the organization consultants;
- senior management; and
- a group that has the responsibility and the knowledge to produce forecasting output.

The panel is exposed, either through a questionnaire or in the form of an extended interview, to questions designed to form the basis for the forecasting activity. Usually the forecast is produced, after several meetings and as a result of argument, discussion and deliberation. The critical task in this method is the development of a group's consensus based on different opinions. However, it has been observed that rank and hierarchy, and not necessarily knowledge, have a great impact on the forecast. Discussion is used to highlight certain situations, and the net contributions of individuals are based on "trait characters" and "corporate influence". Indeed, the very strength of a panel is the differences among the participants. When these differences are based on "areas of work" and "specialization", the quality of the results obtained is enhanced. However, when differences reflect only rank levels, forecasts may only be a projection of management objectives.

To avoid some of these problems the panel consensus method can be supplemented by quantitative estimates as in the case of the following example:

"An investment group is evaluating the financial profitability of building a hotel in Happytown. A key information in this assessment is a forecast of future levels of occupancy."

Applying the panel consensus method would require the selection of a group of experts, say ten, who would first be provided by some basic facts about the characteristics of the area including the performance of the regional lodging industry. After discussions and an exchange of opinions, each expert would register his vote. For the individuals who assessed the need for a hotel to be positive, a level of occupancy is registered. Eight experts agree that there is a demand for a new hotel in Happytown whereas two experts believe that there is no evidence to support a need for a hotel. Three levels of occupancy were proposed and the eight experts selected the most probable rate of occupancy. For instance,

- The rate of occupancy is high (80%) = 2 experts, or 25%,
- The rate of occupancy is average (65%) = 5 experts, or 62.5%,
- The rate of occupancy is low (40%) = 1 expert, or 12.5%.

Assuming that each rate of occupancy is associated with a level of expected revenues (Price x number of rooms x rate of occupancy), an "average revenue" can be estimated based on the experts' forecasts. Expected revenues are shown in Table 2.1.

TABLE 2.1
EXPECTED REVENUES
HAPPYTOWN HOTEL

Rate of occupancy	Expected revenues (million $)	Probability of occurrence	Probable revenues (million $)
80%	5	(.8) x (.250) = .200	($5) (.200) = $1
65%	4	(.8) x (.625) = .500	($4) (.500) = $2
40%	2	(.8) x (.125) = .100	($2) (.100) = $0.2
0%	0	(.2) x (1.000) = .200	($0) (1.000) = $0
			$3.2

Given the responses provided by the panel of experts, the expected revenues of the Happytown Hotel amount to $3.2 million.

In some situations, the panel is a "fixed" sample consisting of the same members who do not necessarily possess a certain knowledge of the subject at hand. Their selection is based solely on the fact that they are representatives of a segment of the population (e.g., seniors, working mothers, teenagers). They are recruited to respond to a product or a service, and it is assumed that their reactions to changes introduced in the product/service reflect their basic socio-economic differences.

2.6.2 EVALUATION

The main advantages of the method are:

.   its rapidity in reaching a solution and its facility in clarifying "grey areas" due to the physical presence of several staff members who have a different perspective on the problem;

.   the exchange of views often leads to reactions and answers that can in turn stimulate discussions and give rise to new ideas and unexpected solutions;

.   the low management and production costs;

.   the fact that few data are needed;

.   the structure to take advantage of individuals who possess knowledge in the area; and

.   bringing individuals from various disciplines and positions together increases the amount of relevant information available to the forecaster.

The main disadvantages of this method are:

.   too much weight is often given to the opinions of certain individuals. This situation creates a bias, even if these individuals possess an excellent knowledge. Timid individuals, regardless of their level of competence, usually have little influence on the group. Thus, the forecast may turn out to be very similar from that of the strongest personality working alone, and the person with the best insight may not carry sufficient weight to sway the whole group decision;

. when the panel is comprised of "senior" management participants, the method consumes too much time because they often take too long to reach a consensus;

. there are no feedback or correction mechanisms; and

. when participants are facing group discussions, the "opinion of the group" is often less accurate than the "average" of the opinions of all participants. This bias is introduced by the following factors:

- the influence of dominant participants who polarize the discussion and orient the group's opinion;
- pressures to reach conformity and social acceptance; and
- material difficulties, such as time constraints and noise.

To avoid erroneous opinions and ensure a clear understanding of the problem, it is suggested that members of the panel be provided with some "basic facts" related to the area of study. Sometimes one or two members are selected and entrusted with the task of being "the devil's advocate" to reduce the influence of other members on the group's opinion. Some improvements can also be gained when the group meetings are well designed and well structured.

2.7 DELPHI METHOD

"The schooling system pays too much attention to learning what was known and too little to finding out about what was not known".

Anonymous

2.7.1 STEPS

In central Greece at Phocides, 600 meters above the waters of the Corinthian Gulf, is an ancient temple where Pythia, the high priestess of the oracle of Apollo, was consulted: the Delphi Temple. Facing uncertainty, the calamity of gods who threatened and protected them, and the possibility of future gains, the ancients sought the help of high priests, fortune-tellers, wizards, augurs and prophets. Knowledge of the future was essential, and the oracles appeased the tormented souls.

In the 1960s, a group of researchers under the leadership of Olaf Helmer and Norman Dalkey of the Rand Corporation, used the Delphi name to describe a qualitative forecasting method. Initially, the method was designed for long-term forecasts where historical data was non-existent, or only partially available.

The objective of the method is to bring together in a logical, unbiased and systematic way, all information related to a particular topic in order to obtain a consensus of opinion.

More specifically, the following six steps are required to attain an average opinion:

1) Define a problem in precise terms. For example: "When do you expect enrolment in fitness clubs to reach 15 percent of the total adult population?" "By what year do you believe the workweek will be reduced to 30 hours?"

2) Form an expert panel, preferably composed of individuals from different disciplines, who are not physically in contact with each other. Their identity is not known to each other and they may reside in distant geographical areas.

3) Distribute to the expert panel a questionnaire that deals with the problem at hand. In some cases, computers are used as a linkage device between members of the panel.

4) Compile the answers of the panel, and calculate the median or mean of each question.

5) Send the questionnaire a second time to members of the panel, indicating the median value of each question as well as their own response. In the light of the group's median responses, members can modify their initial response.

6) Repeat the same process until the median ceases to be altered or a point of diminishing return is reached. The group is not explicitly asked to reach a consensus, and the statistical median or mean represents the group's final opinion. In general, the iterative process and the group's median answers usually lead to a certain consensus in the opinions of the members of the panel. Thus, the end product is the consensus of experts, including their commentaries, which are usually organized in a written report.

2.7.2 EVALUATION

The method is used for "medium" and "long-term" projections. The rationale of the method is based on three possibilities vis-à-vis the future:

.   a total knowledge of the future, in which case there is no need to forecast;

- speculation; and

- informed opinion.

This "informed opinion" is preferred over pure speculation. Moreover, two premises underlie the Delphi method:

- Persons who are experts in their field make the most plausible forecasts; and

- The combined knowledge of several persons is at least as good or better than that of one person.

The quality of the results obtained by this method depends essentially on the capacity to overcome problems such as:

The questionnaire

Questions must be clear and their interpretation by different experts must be similar. Any ambiguous questions should be removed, since unconditional statements could only diminish the value of the results. However, problems may arise in accurately explaining the situation and the objective of each question and what the expert is required to do.

Results interpretation

Statistical compilation may convey the illusion of precision even if the results do not allow it. Thus, results should not be over-classified and organized quantitatively, and the experts should be permitted to interpret the information in its original form. In some situations, the results are manipulated voluntarily or involuntarily. Moreover, ranking qualitative answers from experts may be a difficult task.

The selection of experts

The selection of experts is central to this method, and the quality of the forecast depends on the criteria used for panel selection. The major difficulty rests in the definition of "expert". To reduce this problem, for each question each panelist must register his own level of expertise. Results can then be weighted by the level of expertise. To avoid confusion in this area, panelists must:

- possess a certain minimum level of knowledge in the investigated area;
- demonstrate, based on previous work, a capability to work in interdisciplinary groups;
- have the capability to align the present with the future;
- possess the ability to adapt to new ideas with a minimum number of preconceived opinions about the problem at hand; and
- have an original approach, and be receptive to new ideas.

Used in cases where only qualitative information is available, this method leads to quantitative estimates based on certain factual evidence and the opinion of informed experts. Among the advantages of the method, one can note the following:

1)   The technique presents an advantage over the single questionnaire approach. It has all the advantages of a questionnaire (it is, in fact, a questionnaire) and it provides participants with the possibility to reassess their answers in the light of the group's responses.

2)   The anonymity of the Delphi responses hinders the influence of conflicts of all kinds. The only indirect influence that the participant is exposed to is the "group's opinion" and, for some questions, the participant can still decide not to take it into consideration.

3) The cost to administer this method is fairly low as compared to personal interviews, meetings or any other method. It economizes on time and money.

4) The method encourages innovative thinking and avoids "tunnel vision" and "bandwagon thinking". It removes the effects of status and group pressures and the influence of dominant individuals.

5) It allows the participation of a larger number of people than would be feasible for group meetings.

6) It saves on management time by reducing the time required to solve certain problems through lengthy meetings.

7) The cost of augmenting the number of participants is marginal.

8) The method facilitates the change of opinion, promotes the multiplicity of views and offers access to expert opinions from a diversified field of knowledge.

9) Properly selected and questioned, a group of experts is often more effective as a forecasting source than an individual forecaster or even an unstructured group of forecasters trying to come up with a consensus on a future issue.

10) In some situations, experts might refuse to participate in a direct exchange, due to timing and location conflicts. In a Delphi method, these difficulties are not applicable.

2.7.3   LIMITATIONS

However, the Delphi method has some built-in limitations, such as:

1)   Forecasts are often so imprecise that it is difficult to determine whether a forecast has been accurate or inaccurate.

2)   By forcing a consensus, it suppresses extreme points of view that may, in the final analysis, be correct.   Convergence of the group estimates is almost invariably observed. However, the critical issue is whether the movement is toward the true value.

3)   Although the method often claims superiority of anonymous group opinion over group and face-to-face discussions, it lacks the stimulation of personal contact.

4)   The method might give an illusion of precision; the results are often misrepresented due to the impression that Delphi is a scientific measurement. In fact, it is nothing more than a system for group conjecture and brainstorming.

5)   The experts generally alter their responses somewhat when they read the responses of their colleagues. After enough rounds, the opinions usually converge into a simple identifiable forecast.

6)   Some participants do not return the questionnaire on time.

7)   Questionnaires are sometimes filled out improperly or incompletely.

8)   It has been often difficult to evaluate the accuracy of the Delphi method because the technique has been used primarily for long-range predictions and not enough time has passed to test their validity.

9)   It confuses aggregations of raw opinions with systematic prediction.

10)   The forecast includes little or no explicit theory. The only theory is the mental model of the forecasters.

2.7.4   IMPROVEMENTS

While the Delphi Method has several shortcomings, it is still an efficient method that yields quite acceptable results. The following suggestions can be made to improve the method:

.   Avoid questions of the type "Are you for or against?", "Are you in agreement or in disagreement with?".

.   Encourage experts to support and explain their positions.

.   Supplement Delphi with a "face-to-face meeting" of the experts.

.   Obtain individual forecasts from each "expert" and combine them using some method of weighting. Four methods are possible:

        -       use equal weights if the level of expertise is believed to be the same;
        -       use weights that are proportional to a subjective assessment of expertise;
        -       use weights that are proportional to a self-assessment of expertise; or
        -       use weights that are proportional to the relative accuracy of past forecasts.

The choice among these methods must rest with the judgement of the management in each specific situation.

2.8 STUDY QUESTIONS

1) What is a Qualitative Forecast Method? What kind of planning situations might precipitate its use? Give several sport and/or recreational planning examples where this method would be particularly appropriate.

2) The treasurer of Northern Ski Shops has been asked to forecast the level of sales, expenses and profits for the next year. Develop a forecasting scenario for the forecasting exercise, using the "Expert Method".

3) Last year attendance at Winterfest dropped by 50 percent. The organizers of the event blamed the bad weather for this mediocre performance and decided not to use a sophisticated econometric model to forecast attendance for next year. The "Expert Method" appeared very promising. What should the management of Winterfest do to apply this method?

4) Rate of occupancy at the Cozy Inn Hotel has been steadily improving over the past five years and management is considering an expansion of the present facilities. A consultant was retained to assess the viability of the project and to forecast future levels. He suggested to apply the "Expert Method". How will he proceed?

5) In the past six months, the manager of "Roll & Bowl" has noticed a major decrease in profits and customer attendance. He has considered having a Bowl-a-Thon for all the leagues. By using the "Expert Method", forecast the probability of this outcome for future purposes.

6) At The Horse Rental Resort, business has been booming and management decided to raise the price of each horse (according to their breed) in order to maintain the rentals and increase his profits. How can the "Expert Method" be applied in this situation?

7) At Springfield Golf Country Club, the majority of the members are Caucasian. The owner wants to integrate different ethnic groups to raise his profits and ethnicity attendance. If the owner were to have some sort of a fund-raising campaign or a new membership price, explain how the "Expert Method" would help forecast the future state of the club.

8) The owner of the Skydome is considering enlarging the seating capacity because of uprises in the sales receipts. Describe and analyze the processes of forecasting future attendance, using the "Expert Method".

9) Name three types of forecasts which may be obtained from experts. Using a wheelchair marathon as an example, indicate the form the forecast would take for each of the three types.

10) What is the Logical Estimates Method? When should it be used in forecasting? Give some examples to illustrate your answer.

11) Parks Canada, a government organization in charge of 46 national parks, decides to use the "Aggregation Method" to forecast attendance at its parks. Describe the process and suggest ways to improve the forecasting results.

12) Best Sports has 16 stores. Management in the head office has been using the "Aggregation Method" to forecast sales. Explain this application of the method.

13) Physiconsult Ltd. was retained by 10 universities to project the future level of enrolment in their Physical Education departments. Physiconsult decided to apply the "Aggregation Method". Describe the method, using a numerical example.

14) The Silver Fitness Club has four locations in the same city. Management wants to know the overall sales for the coming year. Using the "Aggregation Method" explain how you would determine the overall sales for the four clubs and suggest ways to improve it.

15) A camp counsellor wants to use the "Aggregation Method" to forecast total attendance of toddlers at a weekend day camp. Describe the processes involved.

16) There is an annual charity baseball game in your city. Using the "Aggregation Method", forecast future attendance of the various leagues for the event.

17) Name several advantages and disadvantages of using the Panel Consensus Method.

18) By using the "Panel Consensus Method", explain how can the Education Board choose a sport that would be more physically suitable for high school students between ages of 15 and 18.

19) The municipal government is trying to decide what type of new sporting leagues it should allow into the community. By using the "Panel Consensus Method", discuss how the panel could reach a sound decision.

20) Describe the steps involved when using the Nominal Group Method. Use the example of designing a new playground for a private daycare facility.

21) Use the Delphi method to predict changes in sports popularity in the year 2010.

22) Which social changes will have higher impact on the pursuit of leisure activities? Apply the Delphi Method to establish a relationship between social changes and leisure.

23) Rank North American preference for the following recreational activities for the year 2010:

- jogging;
- cycling;
- swimming;
- boating; and
- skiing.

2.9 BIBLIOGRAPHY

BEST, R.
1974 "An Experiment in Delphi Estimation in Marketing Decision Marketing", *Journal of Marketing Research*, Vol. 11, 448-452.

BOUCHER, R.L.
1980 Forecasting for Intramural and Recreational Program: the Delphi Approach, *Journal of National Intramural-Recreational Sports Association*, 4 (3), 22-25.

BROCKHOFF, K.
1984 "Forecasting Quality and Information", *Journal of Forecasting*, Vol. 3 (4), 417-428.

BUNN, D. and G. WRIGHT
1991 "Interaction of Judgemental and Statistical Forecasting Methods: Issues and Analysis", *Management Science*, Vol. 37 (5), 501-518.

CHAI, D.X.
1977 Future of Leisure: A Delphi Approach, *Research Quarterly*, 48 (3), 518-524.

CLEARY, J.P.
1982 *The Professional Forecaster: The Forecasting Process Through Data Analysis*, Belmont, CA: Lifetime Learning Publications.

D'AGOSTINO, R.B.
1975 "Social Indicators: A Statistician's View", *Social Indicators Research*, Vol. 1 (4), 459-484.

DALKEY, N.C.
1967 *Experiments in Group Prediction*, Paper P-3829, Santa Monica, CA: Rand Corporation.

DALKEY, N.C.
1968 *Predicting the Future*, Paper P-3948, Santa Monica, CA: Rand Corporation.

DALKEY, N. and O. HELMER
1963 "An Experimental Application of the Delphi Method to the Use of Experts", *Management Science*, April, 458-467.

DIETZ, T.
1987 "Methods for Analyzing Data from Delphi Panels: Some Evidence from a Forecasting Study", *Technological Forecasting and Social Change*, Vol. 31 (1), 79-85.

ELLIS, G., K. SMITH and W.G. KUMMER
1985 A Delphi Approach to Curriculum Planning, *Parks and Recreation*, 20 (9), 52-57.

FAIRCHILD MARKET RESEARCH DIVISION
1984 *The Sports/Fitness/Leisure Markets*, New York, NY: Fairchild Publications.

HARRIS, T.R., G.S. EVANS and K. RAFFIEE
1991 "The Need for Multiple Information Sources in the formulation of an Economic Development Plan: An Application of Delphi, Community, and Executive Survey Techniques", *Journal of the Community Development Society*, Vol. 22 (2), 47-67.

HAWKINS, D.I.
1992 *Consumer Behavior-Implications for Market Strategy*, Homewood, IL: Irwin.

HELMER, O.
1977 "Problems in Futures Research, Delphi and Causal Cross-Impact Analysis", *Futuribles*, Vol. 9 (1), 17-31.

HOGARTH, R.M.
1982 "Prediction, Diagnosis, and Causal Thinking in Forecasting", *Journal of Forecasting*, Vol. 1, 23-36.

HOLLOMAN, C. and H. HENDRICK
1972 "Adequacy of Group Decisions as a Function of the Decision-Making Process", *Academy of Management Journal*, Vol. 15, 175-184.

HUDDLESTON, J.
1989 "Evaluating an Application of Computer-Based Delphi Techniques to Narrative Futures Exploration", *Futures Research Quarterly*, Vol. 5 (3), 71-80.

LINSTONE, H.
1975 *The Delphi Method: Techniques and Applications*, Reading, Mass: Addison Wesley Publishing Company.

MILLER, D.A.
1990 Research through the Delphi Technique, *N.I.R.S.A. Journal*, 15 (1), 39-40.

MOELLER, G.H.
1975 Delphi Technique: An Approach to Identifying Events that will Shape the Future of Outdoor Recreation, In *Proceedings - National Research Symposium - Indicators of*

Change in the Recreation Environment, University Park, PA: Pennsylvania State University.

MOELLER, G.H. and E.L. SHAFER
1987   The Delphi Technique: A Tool for Long-range Tourism and Travel Planning, Ch 34 of Ritchie J.R.B., and Goeldner, C.R. (eds.) *Travel, Tourism and Hospitality Research*, New York: John Wiley, 417-424.

MOELLER, G.H. and E.L. SHAFER
1983   The Usc and Misuse of Delphi Forecasting, In Lieber, S.R. and D.R. Fesenmaier (eds.), *Recreation Planning and Management*, State College, PA: Venture Publishing Inc., 96-104.

MUMPOWER, J.L., S. LIVINGSTON and T.J. LEE
1987   "Expert Judgements of Political Riskiness", *Journal of Forecasting*, Vol. 6, 51-66.

MUNTZING, U.
1989   *Predicting Future Trends in Elementary Physical Education using the Delphi Technique*, Eugene, OR: Microfilm Publications.

MURRAY, W.F. and B.O. JARMAN
1987   Predicting Future Trends in Adult Fitness using the Delphi Approach, *Research Quarterly for Exercise and Sport*, 58 (2), 124-131.

PARENTÉ, F.J., J.K. ANDERSON, P. MYERS and T. O'BRIEN
1984   "An examination of Factors Contributing to Delphi Accuracy", *Journal of Forecasting*, Vol. 3, 173-182.

RAUCH, W.
1979   "The Decision Delphi", *Technological Forecasting and Social Change*, Vol. 15 (3), 159-169.

ROWE, G., G. WRIGHT and F. BOLGER
1991   "Delphi: A Reevaluation of Research and Theory", *Technological Forecasting and Social Change*, Vol. 39 (3), 235-251.

SALANICK, J.R., W. WENGER, and E. HELFER
1971   The Construction of Delphi Event Statements, *Technological Forecasting and Social Change*, 3, 65-73.

SHIMIZU, J.K.
1991   *Tourism Forecasting and Delphi Technic: A Case Study*, University of Oregon: Microform Publications.

TASHAKORI, A, J.H. BARNES, Jr. and G.E. LYNE
1988   "The Future of U.S. Free Enterprise: A Delphi Study", *Futures Research Quarterly*, Vol. 4, 29-42.

VANDIJK, J.A.
1990   "Delphi Questionnaires Versus Individual and Group Interviews: A Comparison Case", *Technological Forecasting and Social Change*, Vol. 37 (3), 293-304.

WEAVER, T.W.
1969   *Delphi as a Method for Studying the Future: Testing Some Underlying Assumptions*, Syracuse University School of Educational Policy Research Centre.

WINKLER, R.L.
1968   "The Consensus of Subjective Probability Distributions", *Management Science*, B: 61-75.

WOUNDENBERG, F.
1991   "An Evaluation of Delphi", *Technological Forecasting and Social Change*, Vol. 40 (2), 131-150.

ZEIGLER, E.F. and J. CAMPBELL
1984   *Strategic Market Planning: An Aid to the Evaluation of an Athletic/Recreation Program*, Champaign, IL: Stipes Publishing Co.

3

MARKET FORECASTING METHODS

*"I don't make jokes: I just watch the Government
and report the facts".*

Will Rogers

3.1 THE MARKET

"Nothing happens unless the cash register rings".

Anonymous

The market can be defined as the meeting place between producers and consumers. Products and services are offered, and prices are influenced by a host of variables ranging from "production costs" to "psychological attitudes". While imperfections are known to disturb the competition process, there is no doubt that the market can still be considered as a highly useful tool to provide the right signals for future changes. Consumer tastes and needs can be obtained through "market information". Such information may include: profile of participants, type of activities, place of residence, willingness to pay, etc. All these variables play an important role in shaping the future. For example:

- the users' willingness to pay has a clear impact on "future" users' charges;
- the market penetration of younger golf players will exert pressures on existing facilities and will give rise to high levels of demand in the future; and
- better eating habits and the use of outdoor activities would have a positive influence on future recreational participation rates.

Information obtained via the market is not only highly useful in projecting the future, but it is often one of the few ways to acquire recent data on consumer habits, users' satisfaction or participants' intentions. If the future stands a good chance to, at least, partially resemble the present, then market surveys should be considered as a firm basis for forecasting purposes.

Moreover, historical data are often not up-to-date and do not always reflect "today's" consumer needs and attitudes. Market data can supplement existing information and establish a bridge between past trends and present levels of demand.

3.2 OPINION SURVEYS

"...what the analyst apparently ignored was that much of the sale of Coke was to people who drank five to six cans per day and that these people, the 'Coke junkies', did not prefer the new Coke... A massive research campaign was foiled by a simple (in retrospect) mistake".

Anonymous

Because participation is measured only for activities in which people currently engage, there is considerable opportunity for mistakes in knowing what people actually desire. People will only participate in activities for which facilities are available. Measurement of participation does not necessarily indicate what they might really want to do. This is one of the serious consequences of mistaking recreation participation for recreation demand and confusing needs with consumption. This bias can be partly reduced by "surveying" participants' needs and treating the signals given by individuals as an indication of their present and future needs.

Opinion surveys assume that the future will partly depend on what people presently believe or plan for the future. They imply that individuals do possess a reasonably accurate basis for foreseeing the future. This assumption directly or indirectly stems from the following observations:

. There is a relationship between present and future habits, needs and demands; and

By expressing an opinion on future demand, the public is implicitly making a commitment.

In the area of sports and recreation, opinion surveys use structured questionnaires which comprise questions related to the forecasted area. The following example, related to *"forecasting the demand for an indoor swimming pool at Bonneville"*, highlights the main segments of a questionnaire. Basically the questionnaire should contain questions related to the following elements:

- Socio-economic profile of the potential users;
- Present aquatic recreational activities of the respondents;
- Support of the project; and
- Expected levels and characteristics of utilization of the future indoor pool.

While it is beyond the scope of this book to review the design of forecasting questionnaires, a few remarks will be made to ensure that questionnaires serve their intended purpose and give rise to minimum bias. Thus:

1) The number of questions should be kept to a minimum. The objective of the questionnaire should be reviewed, and only questions which have significance to the forecast should be included. Too many questions will lead to respondent's fatigue and reduce the enthusiasm of the respondent to answer the questions. Questions which have little or no reliance must be avoided.

2) Questions must be short and clear. The longer the question, the harder it is to understand.

3) Offensive questions should be avoided. For example, questions concerning an individual's private life, confidential information or security facts have usually a marginal impact on the forecast and negatively affect the attitude of the respondent.

4)	Influential or leading questions should not be used. This approach does not yield answers free of constraints and true answers may not be obtained. For instance, questions such as the following should be avoided:

"Do you agree that pollution should be discouraged and a special tax should be imposed on motor boats?"

5)	Questions should be easy to answer and require simple answers. Avoid:

.	Technical terms: *"Future rate structures should reflect only fixed costs"*.
.	Double-barrelled questions: *"Hockey players' project a violent image of sports and hockey player's salaries should be lower"*.

Thus, in the area of forecasting, surveys are quite powerful tools and provide the forecaster with accurate information at relatively low cost if they are properly designed and administered. However, the forecaster should:

.	ensure that the survey will provide the required information;

.	present the survey as a beneficial tool to the respondent. If there is no incentive for the respondent to answer truthfully, then the results might be biased. Often, respondents will give wrong signals simply to serve their purpose e.g. hoteliers will estimate upward the number of tourists in the hope that their "prophecy" will be self-fulfilling;

.	develop the questions in a way that will explain to the respondents their options. For instance, if government wishes to introduce a user's fee and only the following question was asked:

***"Are you in favour of a user's fee?"*,**

the answers would not reflect the reality if the absence of a fee would mean cutting down the services offered. The survey should include a question explaining the impact and implications of a rejection of user's fees.

- select the right words. The choice of words is important. For instance, in predicting tourist arrivals during the summer session, a forecaster may ask in April about intentions to take a vacation during the summer:

> *"Do you expect to take a vacation ...."*
> *"Do you plan ...."*
> *"Do you intend ...."*
> *"Are you taking ...."*

The accuracy of the forecast is highly affected by the answers given to the above four questions. The difference between "expectations" and "actual purchase" of a plane ticket clearly affects the accuracy of forecasting the level of tourist activity.

For forecasting purposes, surveys may be used to determine preferences, attitudes, habits, willingness to pay, choices, etc. Once these dimensions are well identified, they can in turn be used to project future demand and the dimensions which should be taken into account in forecasting the future environment. Consider the following example:

Springborough's residents are asking the Parks and Recreation department to add a pool to the existing two pools. If a survey is carried out to forecast future needs, most likely the following information will be obtained:

- a large percentage of the population will respond favourably to the need for an additional pool;
- most people will suggest that if the pool is built, they will use it; and
- again, the majority would not favor additional taxes to support this project.

How can the forecaster use the information contained in the survey to "forecast future demand"? There is no doubt surveys could provide false signals. Future participation cannot simply be based on general market responses. When individuals are not constrained by specific actions, they would tend to exaggerate their real demand. In this case the survey will be more helpful in areas such as:

- changes in consumer tastes;

- most desirable type of pool (recreational pool, sports oriented pool, diving pool, wave-tech pool etc...);

- present rate of utilization; and

- need for an aquatic program.

3.2.1 EVALUATION

Market surveys are widely used for several reasons:

. they allow us to solicit information directly from a particular interest group;

. they provide information on consumers' feedback and how they respond to future change;

. they assist in setting priorities to different variables; and

. they are relatively easy to administer and provide access to a valued resource bank.

On the other hand, market surveys present some weaknesses, namely:

.   sometimes, results reflect how respondents felt they should respond and not how they truly feel;

.   results are often inconclusive;

.   exogenous variables (i.e. timing, climate) may affect the answers obtained;

.   sample population is not always representative of actual population; and

.   individuals would tend to give false signals in order not to be denied the future right to use recreational facilities. For instance, if a survey is used to forecast the demand for a bowling alley, people would tend to suggest that they will use the facility even if, at present, they do not participate in this game.

3.3 LONGITUDINAL SURVEYS

"Every ten years the United States is invaded... For the goal of this army is to collect the detailed intelligence on which millions of business decisions will be based ... The organization involved is, of course, the U.S. Bureau of the Census..."

Alvin Toffler

Longitudinal surveys have useful applications in forecasting participation rates. Reliability of forecasts is highly sensitive to changes in participation rates, and a better knowledge of the rates highly improves the accuracy of the forecast. Indeed, if one considers that total number of participants is the product of:

Participation rate x Population,

then it becomes obvious that the forecasting error is more related to participation rates then it is to the level of population. If participation rates are unstable, then the total number of participants will be difficult to forecast. To alleviate this problem and shed more light on participation rates, longitudinal surveys can be used. Respondents are asked if they did or did not participate in various activities over a given year and are classified according to certain socio-economic characteristics such as income, age, marital status, number of children at home, place of residence, etc.. Participation rates are then associated with socio-economic characteristics to establish specific participation rates for each subgroup of the population.

Total forecast is obtained by projecting the population of each socio-economic subgroup, multiplying the group-specific participation rates by the expected numbers of persons in each subgroup, and summing over all subgroups. However, the assumption that participation rates within subgroups will remain stable, limits the validity of this approach. This bias can be corrected by longitudinal surveys in the following way:

.   conduct a survey every 5 years using the same"cohort";

.   during that period, register major changes in the socio-economic characteristics of the cohort as well as changes in participation rates;

.   relate both changes; and

.   forecast future levels of the socio-economic variables, and use these levels to project future participation rates.

3.4 DIRECT INTERVIEWS

"The lion said: nobody will look after my business as myself".

Arab Proverb

Direct interviews are often used to forecast future needs. The method suggests that the person who is most familiar with a system and so, theoretically at least, most qualified to forecast, is the person who uses it and works with it. For this reason, interviews, as forecasting tools, aim at obtaining first hand information about future levels of activity. Consider the following examples:

- Interview the general manager of a recreation program to forecast future levels of participation,

- Interview an official of the National Football Association to predict future salaries of football players,

- Interview the president of the Tourism Bureau to forecast the future level of tourism demand, or

- Interview the director of the Hotel Industry Association to forecast future levels of hotel occupancy.

In all cases, the aim is to obtain information related to a specific area from individuals who are "experts" in this area. However, collecting valid opinions is a tricky business and can easily yield deceptive information. The art of asking good questions is one which very few people master. Some ways of asking questions give results which, for all practical purposes, are worthless. Questions which are heavily loaded are of no value whatsoever. Consider the following wording:

"Why is this program offered despite the high level of dissatisfaction?"

The fundamental question is the validity of the interview as a "forecasting tool". To ensure the reliability of the information obtained, the following guidelines are suggested:

i) the interviewer should express the question in such a fashion that the respondent can easily understand it;

ii) the interviewer may probe more deeply, in order to obtain more adequate interpretation of the answers to each question or to test or check another answer; and

iii) the interviewer must become alert to what he is bringing in to the interview situation (e.g. appearance, gestures, intonation...).

Interviewing is essentially a process of social interaction and some individuals in a social group seem to understand the dislikes and likes of the rest better than others do. Their answers would reflect this fact and might bias the quality of the forecast. For this reason, interviews oriented towards forecasting should be reasonably well structured, in order to reduce deviations due to emotions, subjectivity or behavioral attitudes. However, this "standardization" should not exclude probing which allows the interviewer to obtain "qualitative" information on the determinants of the forecasts. In fact, interviews are often more appropriate for understanding the forecasting environment and the forces shaping up the forecast, than obtaining precise figures on the forecasted variable.

3.5 STUDY QUESTIONS

1) Construct three separate questionnaires dealing with forecasting:

   - tourist arrivals (next 3 years);
   - popularity of professional sports; and
   - growing costs of recreation delivery.

2) Provide some examples of:

   - offensive questions; and
   - leading questions.

3) How can a survey be used to forecast for example, the demand for bicycle paths in a specific community?

4) List 5 precautionary measures to be taken when designing questionnaires.

5) What would be the advantages and disadvantages of surveying high school students for their opinions on the future need for outdoor basketball courts?

6) What is the main problem confronting longitudinal surveys?

7) How would a Longitudinal Survey technique be utilized by a city which wants to determine future participation rates of neighborhood wading pools?

8) A senior's recreational facility has had a stable participation rate over the last ten years; management assumes that this will not likely change over the next ten years, especially

since their recent survey of participants indicates a continued participation. By using the Longitudinal Survey technique, how could you avoid a possible bias of assuming a stable participation rate?

9)   Can you combine "opinion surveys" with "direct interviews" to forecast participation in a fitness club? Describe the different steps required to achieve this forecast.

10) Using the Direct Interview technique, make a list of who you would interview (e.g. their job titles, occupation, area of expertise etc.), in order to forecast future participation rates for a region which wanted to hold its own "Mini Special Olympics".

11) State the problems which may arise when using the Direct Interview technique.

12) What would be the error(s) of a survey designed to forecast for example, future participation rates in a football league, if only the current participants were questioned?

3.6 BIBLIOGRAPHY

ASSMUS, G.
1984 "New Product Forecasting", *Journal of Forecasting*, Vol. 3, 121-138.

CHRISTENSEN, J.E.
1982 "On Generalizing About the Need for Follow-up Efforts in Mail Recreation Surveys", *Journal of Leisure Research*, Vol. 14, 263-265.

CICCHETTI, C.J.
1972 "A Review of the Empirical Analyses that have been Based upon the National Recreation Surveys", *Journal of Leisure Research*, Vol. 4, 90-107.

COOPER, R.B.A., A. SOMERSON, N. ENOSH and S. MCKINNEY
1974 Upper Great Lakes Regional Recreation Planning Study, Part 2 *Recreation Demand Survey and Forecasts*, Madison: Recreation Resource Centre, University of Wisconsin Extension.

EICHNER, K., W. HABERMEHL, T.A. HEBERLEIN and R.M. BAUMGARTNER
1981 "Predicting Response Rates to Mailed Questionnaires", *American Sociological Review*, Vol. 46 (3), 361-363.

ESOMAR
1973 *Seminar on Fieldwork: Sampling and Questionnaire Design*, Amsterdam: ESOMAR.

ESOMAR/WAPOR: CONGRESS
1973 *Secondary Analysis of Sample Surveys: Uses and Needs*, Amsterdam: WAPOR.

HAGENAARS, J.A.
1990 *Categorical Longitudinal Data: Log-Linear panel, Trend, and Cohort Analysis*, Newbury Park, CA: Sage Publications.

HYMAN, H.H.
1972 *Secondary Analysis of Sample Surveys: Principles, Procedures, and Potentialities*, New York, NY: Wiley.

JOHNSON, J.R.
1993 *A Survey of Division II Athletic and Physical Education Fiscal Trends for the Next 20 Years*, Eugene, OR: Microfilm Publications.

LaPAGE, W.F. and D.F. RAGAIN
1974   "Family Camping Trends - An Eight - Year Panel Study", *Journal of Leisure Research*, Vol. 6, 101-112.

LIVINGSTONE, J.M.
1977   *A Management Guide to Market Research*, Basingstoke: MacMillan.

MAHMOUD, ESSAM
1989   Combining Forecasts: Some Managerial Issues, *International Journal of Forecasting*, 5, 4, 599-600.

MURDOCK, S.H., K. BACKMAN and Md. N. HOQUE
1991   "The Implications of Change in Population Size and Composition on Future Participation in Outdoor Recreational Activities", *Journal of Leisure Research*, Vol. 23, 238-259.

RITCHIE, J.R.B. AND C.R. GOELDNER, (eds.)
1987   *Travel, Tourism and Hospitality Research*, New York: John Wiley.

TANNY, S.
1984   Forecasting for Survival, In, BANGAY, J. (ed.), *Aquatic Programming: Reaching Today's Market, Proceedings of the 1983 symposium, Ottawa, Ontario*, Toronto, ON: Royal Life Saving Society Canada, 39-41.

WELLMAN, J.D., E.D. HAWK, J.W. ROGGENBUCK and G.J. BUHYOFF
1980   "Mailed Questionnaire Surveys and the Reluctant Respondent: An Empirical Examination of Differences Between Early and Late Respondents", *Journal of Leisure Research*, Vol. 12, 164-173.

WHYTE, D.N.B.
1992   Key Trends and Issues Impacting Local Government Recreation and Park Administration in the 1990s: A focus for Strategic Management and Research, *Journal of Park and Recreation Administration*, 10 (3), 89-106.

WHYTE, W.F.
1991   *Participatory Action Research*, Newbury Park, CA: Sage Publications.

WILSON, G.L. and M.S. HANNA
1990   *Groups in Context: Leadership and Participation in Small Groups*, 2nd. ed. New York, NY: McGraw Hill.

4

NUMERICAL METHODS

"The glass is falling hour by hour, the glass will fall forever, but if you break the bloody glass you won't hold up the weather".

Louis MacNiece

4.1 DEFINITION

"Strictly speaking, one may even say that nearly all our knowledge is problematical".

Laplace

Numerical methods rely simply on some numerical manipulation without any explanation of the underlying variables which shape the forecast. They are simple to apply but they are fixed and do not permit much understanding of the behaviour of the forecasted variable. They usually take the form of:

-    Computing past growth rates and applying a weighted or non-weighted average to future years; and/or

-    Using a standard analysis where the forecasted variable is related to some accepted and commonly understood measure like population.

They are often referred to as "naïve methods". In forecasting, the term "naïve" is usually applied to forecasting methods which solely use historical values of the variables to be forecast. Thus, the forecast is obtained from previous observations of the forecast variable with no attempt to establish a relationship with other variables. The forecaster applying these methods simply proceeds as if the future will resemble the recent past. His behaviour implies that the next period will have similar characteristics as the present or last period.

In general, many time series move in the same direction over successive years. Thus, simple numerical methods, which predict each year the same change based on previous performance, will do very well in terms of average annual absolute percentage error. They will, however, never pick up a turning point.

4.2 PERCENTAGE CHANGE METHOD

"There is nothing so fallacious as facts - except figures".

George Cumming

One of the least complex techniques of forecasting is that of the Percentage Change Method. In essence, this method attempts to evaluate the percentage change in the forecast variable between successive periods of time. Attendance at Bonneville park is used to illustrate this method.

TABLE 4.1

ATTENDANCE AT BONNEVILLE PARK

Year	Attendance	Percentage Change
1	14,880	--
2	16,660	11.96
3	18,470	11.00
4	18,790	1.73
5	20,490	9.00
6	20,300	(1.00)
7	20,290	(0.04)
8	21,720	7.05
9	20,070	(0.76)
10	20,350	1.40
11	20,440	0.44
12	22,010	7.68
13	23,200	5.41
14	22,850	(1.51)
15	24,310	6.39
16	26,400	8.60
17	27,850	5.49
Annual average		*4.55*

When we look ahead to the future, it is not unusual to start by glancing at the past to see where the trends are likely to lead. What Table 4.1 tells us, is that over a period of 17 years the combined effect of several variables have led to an overall increase in attendance of about 4.6 percent annually. This annual growth would in turn be used to forecast future attendance by augmenting attendance by a factor of 4.6 percent per year, as demonstrated in Table 4.2.

TABLE 4.2

**PROJECTED ATTENDANCE
AT BONNEVILLE PARK**

Year	Attendance
year 17 (actual)	27,850
year 18	*29,131*
year19	*30,471*
year 20	*31,873*

The formula used to calculate the percentage rate of change is:

$$\frac{t_1 - t_0}{t_0} \times 100$$

where:

t_0 = base year

t_1 = subsequent year

Sometimes when the trend is reasonably linear, only the first and the last year of the total period are used to calculate the rate of change. For attendance at Bonneville, the rate of change is:

$$\frac{27,850 - 14,880}{14,880} \times 100 = 87.16 \; percent$$

This "overall growth rate" has to be divided by 16 (N-1) to obtain the annual growth rate. N-1 = number of observations less 1, which is also equal to the number of "changes" during the period under consideration.

$$87.16 \div 16 = 5.45 \; percent$$

In this particular situation the second method yields a higher rate of growth due to the acceleration of the growth rate in the last years of the sample (5.45% as compared to 4.55%)

4.2.1 EVALUATION

There are several problems with the use of the Percentage Change Method for forecasting. The first, and perhaps most important, is that a long-term trend may easily be overlooked. By simply computing the average percentage change, the forecast is greater than warranted. If the long-term trend is positive, the percentage change method will tend to overestimate the forecast; conversely if the long-term trend is negative the method will tend to underestimate the forecast. A second limitation, which is also common to most naïve forecasts, is the lack of any "explanatory basis" to project future levels. Past growth may be due to "demand forces" as well as "supply forces" or both. Identifying and separating the dependent variables often has a useful operating role. This is not possible when naïve methods are applied. A third limitation is that recent changes may be more indicative of the future then older data. A fourth limitation is that percentage change method has an upward bias; for example, an observation can drop by 50%, but to it has to grow by 100% increase to its original value.

4.3 WEIGHTED PERCENTAGE CHANGE METHOD

"By Jove, she's got it".

Lerner/Loewe "My Fair Lady"

To overcome the third difficulty indicated in the previous section, namely the importance of more recent changes over older changes, the Weighted Percentage Change Method can be used. The simple percentage change method weighs each historical observation equally in calculating the trend. A fluctuation in a value has the same impact on the computed trend throughout the entire range of periods, whereas a weighed increase is used in the case of a "weighted percentage change".

Using the same data as in Table 4.1 we obtain:

TABLE 4.3

ATTENDANCE AT BONNEVILLE PARK

WEIGHTED PERCENTAGE CHANGE

Years	Attendance	Percentage Change	Weight	Weighted % Change
1	14,880	--	--	--
2	16,660	11.96	1	11.96
3	18,470	11.00	2	22.00
4	18,790	1.73	3	5.19
5	20,490	9.00	4	36.00
6	20,300	(1.00)	5	(5.00)
7	20,290	(0.04)	6	(0.24)
8	21,720	7.05	7	49.35
9	20,070	0.76	8	60.80
10	20,350	1.40	9	12.60
11	20,440	0.44	10	4.40
12	22,010	7.68	11	84.48
13	23,200	5.41	12	64.92
14	22,850	(1.51)	13	(19.63)
15	24,310	6.39	14	89.46
16	26,400	8.60	15	129.00
17	27,850	5.49	16	87.84
			136	633.13

The weighted percentage change is 4.7 percent (633.13 ÷ 136) as compared to 4.6 for the non-weighted. Using the weighted average percentage change to project attendance, we obtain:

TABLE 4.4

PROJECTED ATTENDANCE AT BONNEVILLE PARK

USING WEIGHTED PERCENTAGE CHANGE

Year	Attendance
year 17 (actual)	27,850
year 18	*29,159*
year 19	*30,529*
year 20	*31,964*

As mentioned earlier, the Weighted Percentage Change Method gives more importance to most recent data. This is based on the assumption that the future would resemble more the present or the near past, rather than the far past. The choice of the weights is usually related to the general trend of the time series. In some cases, for instance, when there is an instability in a portion of the trend or a "kink", it may be advisable to use the same weights for that portion of the curve which has the same characteristics. This is illustrated by Figure 4.1:

FIGURE 4.1

TREND IN ATTENDANCE

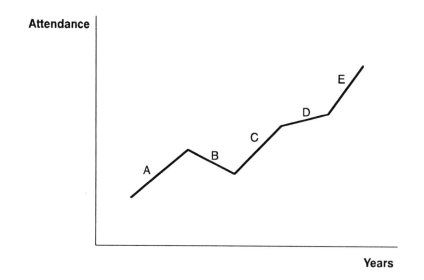

In Figure 4.1, the trend may be segmented into five segments which have different slopes and different rates of change. It would then be advisable that for each segment the weight remain the same. Moreover, if the forecaster has reasons to believe that the future will resemble more to segment (A) or (D), then higher weights should be given to the annual rate of change in (A) or (D).

4.3.1 EVALUATION

While the Weighted Percentage Change Method offers a better basis to project the future, it still has most of the weaknesses inherent in the Percentage Change Method discussed in the previous section (4.2.1). Moreover, often the choice of the weights is arbitrary and could lead to serious biases if recent changes do not have a higher probability to materialize in the future.

4.4 RATIO METHOD

"In spite of its triviality, this circumstance should not be overlooked".

J. Von Neumann

The Ratio Method is a static measure of the proportion of one variable to another. Essentially it relates the variable to be forecasted to a larger denominator like land, population, or income. This method is used only when the variations in the forecasted variable are larger than the variations in the related variable so that the ratio of the two variables has a more stable pattern. Using data on attendance at Bonneville Park (Table 4.5), the regional population around Bonneville Park can be used to establish the visits per capita rate.

TABLE 4.5

ATTENDANCE AT BONNEVILLE PARK

RATIO METHOD

Year	Attendance	Population	Ratio (attendance/ population)	Percentage Change in Ratio
1	14,880	12,000	1.24	—
2	16,660	12,200	1.37	10.5
3	18,470	12,220	1.51	10.2
4	18,790	12,450	1.51	0
5	20,490	12,700	1.61	6.6
6	20,300	13,000	1.56	-3.1
7	20,290	13,300	1.53	-1.9
8	21,720	13,625	1.59	3.9
9	20,070	13,900	1.44	-9.4
10	20,350	14,300	1.42	-1.4
11	20,440	14,700	1.39	-2.1
12	22,010	15,100	1.46	5.0
13	23,200	15,500	1.50	2.7
14	22,850	16,000	1.43	-4.7
15	24,310	16,600	1.46	2.1
16	26,400	17,220	1.53	4.8
17	27,850	18,000	1.55	1.3
TOTAL				24.5

Data from the above table will be used to forecast attendance in the following way:

i)   Calculate the average annual rate of change of the ratio (attendance/population). In this case, it amounts to 1.53 percent per year:

Net total change / number of changes = 24.5 / 16 = 1.53

ii)   Project the ratio up to year 20 using the annual rate of change in the ratio.

YEAR	RATIO
17	1.55
18	1.57
19	1.59
20	1.61

iii)   Obtain population forecasts for year 20. In general, demographic forecasts are readily available. Assume year 20 population level is 19,800 using a simple extrapolation method.

iv)   On the basis of the information obtained by the above three steps, attendance for year 20 can be forecasted as follows:

- Ratio (attendance/population), year 20 = 1.61
- Population, year 20 = 19,800
- Attendance, year 20 = 1.61 x 19,800 = 31,878

4.4.1 EVALUATION

The method yields acceptable results when the ratio is comprised of a stable series and a series that shows some fluctuations. Because of their simplicity, "ratios" have been widely used by planners as well as politicians to compare existing facilities on a per capita basis. However, using population is often an arbitrary measure and a certain refinement (e.g. age groups) would improve the forecasting power of the method.

4.5 SEMI-AVERAGES METHOD

"If we draw any smooth curve to represent the general trend of population, the actual figures must necessarily rise sometimes above and sometimes below this mean trend line".

Irving Fisher

The method of semi-averages is a crude measure of establishing a trend line which can in turn be used to estimate future values. This is done by dividing the data into two parts, preferably with the same number of years. (we can make the two parts equal, simply by omitting the middle year). Using data from Table 4.1, a series covering a period of 17 years could be divided into one part going from year 1 to year 8 and the other going from year 10 to year 17. The mean of the quantities making up the series separately for each part will be used to establish a "trend line". This is done by plotting the two means at the mid-points of the time intervals covered by the respective parts, and finally joining these two points with a straight line. This line is the trend line. Using data from Table 4.1 the two means are calculated as follows:

$$\frac{14,880 + 16,660 + 18,470 + 18,790 + 20,490 + 20,300 + 20,290 + 21,720}{8} = 18,950$$

$$\frac{20,350 + 20,440 + 22,010 + 23,200 + 22,850 + 24,310 + 26,400 + 27,850}{8} = 23,426$$

Plotting these two averages at points corresponding to the mid-points of the respective periods and connecting them with a straight line, we obtain a trend line as shown in Figure 4.2. For any given year the value on the line is referred to as the corresponding trend value.

FIGURE 4.2

LINEAR TREND: SEMI-AVERAGES

BONNEVILLE PARK

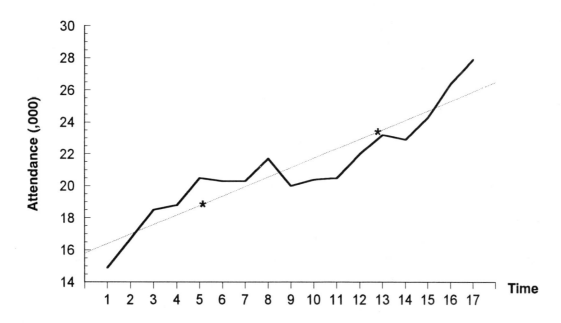

This constructed trend line can be used as a basis for forecasting as follows:

- Calculate the annual trend increment which is the average increase per year. Since the total increase from year 1 to 17 is 12,970 (27,850 - 14,880), the average increase per year is 810.6 (12,970/16).

- Having found this annual trend increment, we can now determine the trend value for any subsequent year. For instance, the value for year 20 can be obtained by augmenting year 17 by three times the annual increase and adding it to attendance level in year 17:

$$810.6 \ x \ 3 = 2,432$$
$$27,850 + 2,432 = 30,282$$

4.5.1 EVALUATION

This method has the advantage of being straightforward and easy to use. However, it is crude and susceptible to distortion by the presence of one or more extreme values and, generally speaking, it is only one step more advanced then drawing a freehand line. When the trend is reasonably linear, the calculated trend line would yield acceptable results. However, the trend of a highly variable time series without any set pattern cannot be captured accurately by this method.

4.6 STUDY QUESTIONS

1)   What does the term "Naive Method" indicate when used in forecasting?

2)   Using the "Percentage Change Method", forecast participation for the years 11 to 15 inclusive for the following three sports activities, as well as for total participation.

TABLE 4.6

SPORT PARTICIPATION, SENIOR HIGH SCHOOL

Year	Basketball	Tennis	Baseball	Total
1	300	90	391	781
2	310	110	410	830
3	340	130	460	930
4	318	115	480	913
5	351	129	505	985
6	359	148	515	1,022
7	410	161	496	1,067
8	430	178	532	1,140
9	440	205	550	1,195
10	428	212	565	1,205

3) A large indoor roller-skating rink has recently used the Percentage Method to forecast future attendance. Data indicates that over the past 10 years attendance has been increasing at a rate of 4% per year. Can management depend on this rate in developing a five-year plan for the future?

4) Apply the "Weighted Percentage Change" to the above data and forecast the years 11 to 15 inclusive.

5) Compare the results obtained by the two methods. Which method do you prefer and why?

6) In which situations does the "Weighted Percentage Change Method" yield better forecasting results?

7) When is it appropriate to use the Ratio Method as a forecasting tool?

8) How can you apply the Ratio Forecast Method to participation data (Table 4.6) at Senior High-School? Project participation for the years 11 - 15 inclusive.

9) Discuss the following statement: "Since a semi-averages straight line is based on mathematical calculations it is always bound to be a more accurate description of linear trend than a freehand line fit to the same data". Use data from suitable published sources to illustrate your argument.

10) Using the Semi-Averages Method and data form the table below:
   (a) construct a "Linear Trend Graph: Semi-Averages";
   (b) calculate the percentage change per year; the "Annual Trend Increment"; and
   (c) determine the "Trend Value" for year 14.

TABLE 4.7
ATTENDANCE AT FRONTIER VILLAGE

Year	Attendance
1	44,300
2	43,600
3	47,200
4	48,100
5	52,700
6	49,200
7	53,500
8	54,200
9	55,800
10	56,200

4.7 BIBLIOGRAPHY

FREUND, J.E. and WILLIAMS F.J.
1958 *Modern Business Statistics*, Englewood Cliffs, NJ: Prentice-Hall.

HENLEY CENTRE
      Henley Centre for Forecasting Leisure Futures, Quarterly, London: Henley Centre.

ROMSA, G.H. and S. GIRLING
1976 "The Identification of Outdoor Recreation Market Segments on the Basis of Frequency of Participation", *Journal of Leisure Research*, Vol. 8, 247-255.

THOMOPOULOS, N.T.
1980 *Applied Forecasting Methods*, Englewood Cliffs, NJ: Prentice-Hall.

WORLD TOURISM ORGANIZATION
1991 *Tourism Trends*, Madrid: World Tourism Organization.

      Travel and Tourism Barometer, Quarterly, Madrid: World Tourism Organization.

5

MATHEMATICAL METHODS

"Mathematics is the science in which we do not know what we are talking about, and do not care whether what we say about it is true".

Bertrand Russell

5.1 SUBJECTIVE PROBABILITY METHOD

"Un homme tirait au sort toutes ses décision. Il ne lui arriva pas plus de mal qu'aux autres qui réfléchissent".

Paul Valery

The subjective or personalistic interpretation of probability was pioneered by L. Savage, R. Schlaifer and H. Raiffa in the early fifties. This school of thought contends that probability is a measure of one's personal belief in a particular outcome or event. For example:

"The chances are 7 to 3 that Mario Lemieux will score more then 80 points during the coming hockey season".

The probability of this event is subjective because various individuals would normally assign different numbers to the odds in favour of, or against the event. Subjective probabilities must satisfy the basic axioms of probability theory, namely:

1)   The probability of any one outcome has a value less than or equal to 1, and greater than or equal to 0.

$$0 \leq p(E_i) \leq 1$$

where E_i (i = 1, 2, ...) is an event in the sample space of the experiment or the situation at hand; and

2)   The probabilities of all possible outcomes in the population must sum to 1.

$$\sum_i P(E_i) = 1$$

The main advantage of subjective probability is that it can be used as a "forecasting tool". This can be done in the following way:

Individuals are asked via a questionnaire or a telephone survey to assign a probability to the future occurrence of an event. For example:

"The number of tourists visiting a particular city per month"

Results of a random survey are tabulated below:

TABLE 5.1

SUBJECTIVE PROBABILITY

TOURIST ARRIVALS

Number of Tourists	Probabilities	Cumulative Probabilities
400,000	0.05	0.05
450,000	0.09	0.14
500,000	0.12	0.26
550,000	0.15	0.41
600,000	0.10	0.51
650,000	0.18	0.69
700,000	0.25	0.94
750,000	0.06	1.00

The cumulative probability can also be shown in a graphical way as a "cumulative distribution function". This function indicates that the subjective probability of tourist arrivals being less than or equal to 750,000 is 1.0. This means that it is certain that the flow of tourist arrivals will not exceed 750,000 tourists. There is a 51 percent probability that arrivals will be less than or equal to 600,000, which is equivalent to saying that there is a 49 percent chance that arrivals will be greater than this amount.

FIGURE 5.1

SUBJECTIVE PROBABILITY

TOURIST ARRIVALS (in thousands)

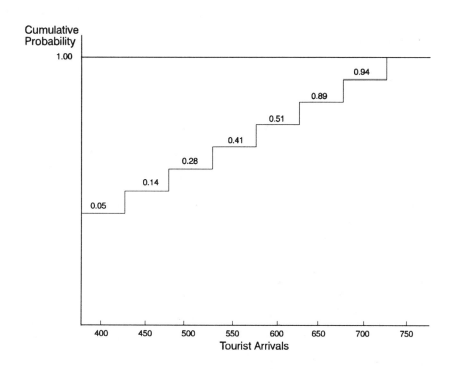

So far we have asked a random sample of "n" individuals only one question (The number of tourists visiting a particular city). This question may be supplemented by the following:

1)   What do you consider to be the "largest possible" number of tourist arrivals for next summer? The largest possible value is defined such that there are 99 chances out of 100 that the "true number of tourists" will be less than or equal to this value.

2)   What do you consider to be the "smallest possible" number of tourist arrivals for next summer? The smallest possible value is defined such that there is only 1 chance in 100 that the "true number of tourists" will be less than this value.

3)   Can you determine the "number of tourist arrivals" based on your answers in (1) and (2)

such that there is a 50-50 chance that the "true" number of tourist arrivals will be above or below this value (median)?

Based on the results of the survey, three "average numbers" were obtained. For the sake of simplicity assume that the survey was addressed to only 10 respondents (N = 10).

TABLE 5.2
TOURIST ARRIVALS
SURVEY RESULTS
(in thousands)

Respondents	Highest	Lowest	Median
1	700	420	600
2	810	500	650
3	750	450	620
4	680	390	500
5	800	525	600
6	700	430	575
7	725	410	600
8	750	475	625
9	740	500	650
10	690	400	580

It should be noted that the "median value" is not the midpoint between the "highest" and the "lowest" figure but the "subjective assessment" of the respondents.

The Subjective Probability Method can be used over a certain period of time and the results obtained can be compared to the "actual levels" in order to improve the forecasting accuracy. The following example compares the "forecasted" and the "actual" values of tourist arrivals.

TABLE 5.3

TOURIST ARRIVALS

ACTUAL AND FORECASTED

(in thousands)

Month	Forecast (F_i)	Actual (A_i)	Forecasting error $(F_i \text{-} A_i)$	$\mid F_i - A_i \mid$
April	450	420	+30	30
May	500	510	-10	10
June	600	640	-40	40
July	625	580	+45	45
August	700	705	- 5	5
September	510	520	-10	10
Average	564	563		

The quality of further forecasts can be improved by using the "previous forecasting" experience. The following relationship will be used:

$$MA\ (measure\ of\ accuracy) = \frac{\sum\limits_{i=1}^{n} \mid Fi - Ai \mid}{n} = \frac{140,000}{6} = 23,333$$

SE = (Measure of the Systematic Error, bias)

$$= \frac{\sum\limits_{i=1}^{n} (F_i - A_i)}{n} = \frac{+\ 10,000}{6} = 1,667$$

CSE = (Correction for Systematic Error)

$$A_i + SE$$

Thus,

Ai		SE		= CSE	Fi		-	CSE		
420,000	+	1667		= 421,667	45,000		-	421,667 =	28,333
510,000	+	1667		= 511,667	500,000		-	511,667 =	11,667
640,000	+	1667		= 641,667	600,000		-	641,667 =	41,667
580,000	+	1667		= 581,667	625,000		-	581,667 =	43,333
705,000	+	1667		= 706,667	700,000		-	706,667 =	6,667
520,000	+	1667		= 521,667	510,000		-	521,667 =	11,667
									143,334

and,

$$MC = \frac{\displaystyle\sum_{i=1}^{n} |F_i - CSE|}{n} = \frac{143,334}{6} = 23,889$$

yields a measure of consistency (MC) after bias has been removed. Results of the above hypothetical example indicate the following:

1)   The measure of consistency is 23,889, representing roughly 4.2 percent of the average number of tourists forecasted. This indicates a fairly good forecasting performance which is also "consistent" over the past 6 months.

2)   This bias (SE) built in the forecasting method is highly acceptable.

5.2 RELEVANCE TREES

"We are surrounded by possibilities that are infinite and the purpose of human life is to grasp as much as we can out of that infinitude".

Alfred North Whitehead

The relevance trees technique starts in the future with an objective or picture of what the future should ideally look like and works back to determine what must occur to make this future happen. The basic objective as well as the sub-objective constitute the relevance tree. Each element is then given relevance weights from which it is possible to calculate the overall relevance. The outcome of the technique is a list of those actions which are needed to attain the higher level objective and sub-objective. Thus, a range of possible desired futures for a specific variable is estimated by the forecaster (or by a panel of experts). The desired future becomes an objective to which the organization strives. Management then has to evaluate the various alternative routes by which the objective can be achieved.

The following example illustrates the use of the method:

i) *Specify main objective:* A panel of experts prepare a scenario of the future which shows "higher levels of physical fitness" as a major objective. This objective will be reached when "at least 50% of individuals 14 years or older participate in a sport-recreational activity".

ii) *Specify sub-objectives. These may include:*

- Public outdoor recreational activities;
- Municipal activities;
- Private sector recreational activities;

. Recreational activities in the educational system; or/and

. Corporate fitness programs.

iii)   *Draw the relevance tree such as in Figure 5.2.* From each sub-objective certain actions can be suggested.

FIGURE 5.2

RELEVANCE TREE EXAMPLE

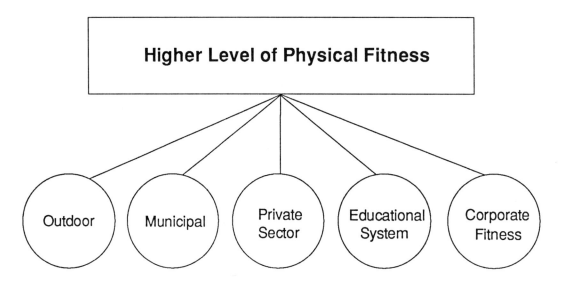

The forecaster now has an idea of the segments which comprise the national objective of higher levels of physical fitness. The experts are asked to identify specific actions related to the relevance tree. These actions may include:

.   more public access to rivers, lakes and seashores;

.   tax transfers to municipalities to develop recreational programs;

.   special funds for fitness clubs;

.   tax allowance for membership fees in private fitness clubs;

- more funds allocated to schools and colleges for sports facilities; and/or

- increase in corporate tax rebate for on-the-job fitness programs.

iv)   *Relevance numbers or weights are assigned by the experts to each element.* The relevance numbers represent the importance of the item in achieving or maximizing the desired objective.

Variables	Weights
. Public access	0.10
. Tax transfers	0.05
. Special funds	0.15
. Tax allowance	0.30
. Funds to educational system	0.25
. Corporate tax rebate	0.15
	1.00

v)   *A final decision is reached.* The forecaster will communicate the weights to the decision makers who in turn will estimate the cost/benefit of each action including its socio-economic, political and environmental impacts.

5.3 CROSS-IMPACT METHOD

"From the physical point of view, the characteristic state of the living organism is that of an open system".

L. von Bertalanffy

This technique is generally used when problems are "fuzzy", that is when they defy precise definition. It is based on the fact that there is an interrelation between certain variables. The cross-impact concept originated with Olaf Helmer and Theodore Gordon in conjunction with the design of a forecasting game for Kaiser-Aluminium, and represented an effort to extend the forecasting techniques of the Delphi Method. In this approach, events were recorded on an orthogonal matrix and at each intersection the question was asked: "If the event in the row were to occur, how would it affect the probability of occurence of the event in the column?" For instance, a shorter workweek (such as the introduction of four-day working week), will have a positive impact on the pursuit of leisure activities. Real world events, of course, do not take place in isolation. When certain events take place they trigger other events. This is the essence of cross-impact analysis. Thus, the occurrence of certain events tend to speed up or hinder other events. The method is based on the formulation of a "cross-impact matrix" which, simply stated, establishes a quantitative relationship between several events. To illustrate the method, the following simple example will be used with particular emphasis on leisure.

TABLE 5.4

CROSS-IMPACT MATRIX

If this event were to occur	*The impact on this event would be*		
	Leisure Time	**User Fees**	**Leisure Activities**
Lower population growth	x_{11}	x_{12}	x_{13}
Higher proportion of elderly	x_{21}	x_{22}	x_{23}
Lower government funding	x_{31}	x_{32}	x_{33}
More household formation	x_{41}	x_{42}	x_{43}
Less working hours	x_{51}	x_{52}	x_{53}

Values have to be assigned to x_{11}, ... x_{53}. Such values can be scaled, say from 0 to 5, where 0 indicates "no impact", and a score of 5 indicates a "high impact". Carried to the next level, the events are given numerical probabilities and the process becomes one in which impacts are measured mathematically. Thus, scales such as the following may be used:

i)   Probability estimates, ranging from 0 to 1; or

ii)   If individuals are not used to thinking in terms of probabilities, a subjective scale may be used, such as:

	Percent
Very likely	90-100
Likely	70-90
As likely as not	50
Not very likely	10-30
Unlikely	0-10

iii)   A simple subjective-numerical scale may also be used:

Impact	Scale
Critical	4
Major	3
Significant	2
Slight	1
No impact	0

From an operational viewpoint the following steps should be followed in making a cross-impact matrix:

1)   Identify a specific problem such as "the four-day work week" and state the length of time as well as the percentage of the labor force which will be working four days per week (e.g. in 10 years 20% of the labor force).

2)   Identify the set of events that are relevant to this problem. These events may include actions, current practices, objectives, decisions etc..., such as higher labor productivity, job sharing, unemployment rate, flexible shopping schedules, women's labor force participation, and leisure pursuit.

3)   Estimate for each event (Ei); the probability (Pi) that it will occur during the time period specified. These estimates are obtained by intuitive judgements by experts, or by extrapolation models if time series data is available.

4)   For each event (Ei) estimate the impact of its occurence (or nonoccurence) on the probabilities of the subsequent occurence of other events. Enter this information in the cross-impact matrix.

Thus, cross-impact analysis attempts to reveal the conditional probability of an event given that various other events have or have not occurred. Sports and recreation events do not occur in isolation but are in some way connected to other events and development. Hence the term "cross-impact" forms something of a Gestalt, and the technique not only forces one to look at the interrelationship between events, but it is also useful as a means of experimenting with ideas to measure their impacts on events. For instance:

- the impact of a four-day work week;
- the introduction of user fees in municipal parks;
- public funding of special events (e.g. carnivals); or
- mandatory retirement at age 60.

One of the key outcomes of cross-impact analysis is the identification of unknown linkages among events. In fact, each of the cell (interactions) can be viewed as a hypothesis for further testing or as a sub-forecast.

5.4 STUDY QUESTIONS

1) Management of a recreation company has to make a decision related to the introduction of a new aquatic sports facility. The decision is not simple and many alternatives may be open to management; examples might include:

- size of the facility;
- location; and/or
- charge to the user.

Apply the "Subjective Probability Method" to predict the expected management decision in relation to the introduction of the aquatic facility.

2) What are the two basic axioms of probability theory?

3) What is a "Relevance Tree"? Illustrate your answer by constructing a relevance tree for the objective: "increase visits to the provincial or state park".

4) Using the relevance tree from "increased visits to the provincial or state park", list several examples of the "specific actions" which may be related to the tree.

5) Develop a "Cross-Impact Matrix" for the following event:
"A major art gallery removes admission charges to all of its main exhibits".

   (a) Identify the set of events that are relevant to this occurrence;
   (b) Estimate for each event (Ei), the probability (Pi) that it will occur during a nine year time period;

(c)   For each event (Ei), estimate the impact of its occurrence (or non-occurrence) on the probabilities of the subsequent occurrence of other events. Enter this information in the cross-impact matrix.

The following information may help you develop the scenario:

Other Art Gallery facilities and events: Pay-for-Parking; Gift Shop; Restaurant; Special Exhibits; Special Noon-hour Performances; Group Lectures; Fund-raising events; "Friends-of-the-Museum" Charity.

6)   Use data from the following table to calculate: the MA; SE; CSE; and MC. Discuss your results.

TABLE 5.5
FORECASTED & ACTUAL ATTENDANCE
KING'S DOME STADIUM
(in thousands)

Month	Forecast (F_i)	Actual (A_i)	Forecasting Error $(F_i - A_i)$	Fi - Ai
May	625	560		
June	900	775		
July	1000	1200		
August	1200	1300		
Sept	900	1000		
Oct	650	600		
Average				

5.5 BIBLIOGRAPHY

CESARIO, F.
1975 "A Simulation Approach to Outdoor Recreation Planning", *Journal of Leisure Research*, Vol. 7, 38-52.

COYLE, G.
1972 *Decision Analysis*, London: Nelson.

EWING, G.O.
1983 Forecasting Recreation Trip Distribution Behavior, In Lieber, S.R. and D.R. Fesenmaier (eds.), *Recreation Planning and Management*, State College, PA: Venture Publishing Inc., 120- .

HAAS, J.D.
1986 "Evaluational Futures: Six Scenarios", *Future Research Quarterly*, Vol. 2, 15-32.

LADANY, S.P. (ed.)
1975 *Management Science Applications to Leisure Time Operations*, Amsterdam: North Holland Pub. Co.

LEVINE, R.L. and W. LODWICK
1983 Introduction to Dynamic Techniques for Forecasting Recreational Behavior, In Lieber, S.R. and D.R. Fesenmaier (eds.), *Recreation Planning and Management*, State College, PA: Venture Publishing Inc., 141-161.

LEVINE, R.L. and W. LODWICK
1983 Continuous Simulation Methodology: A System Dynamics Approach to Planning, Forecasting and Analysis of Recreational Usage, In Lieber, S.R. and D.R. Fesenmaier (eds.), *Recreation Planning and Management*, State College, PA: Venture Publishing Inc., 162-186.

RAIFFA, H.
1968 *Decision Analysis: Introductory Lectures on Choices Under Uncertainty*, Reading Mass: Addison-Wesley.

SAVAGE, L.J.
1954 *The Foundation of Statistics*, New York, NY: John Wiley and Sons, Inc.

SCHECHTER, M. and R.C. LUCAS
1975   *Simulation of Recreational Use for Park and Wilderness Management*, Baltimore: The
        Johns Hopkins University Press.

SCHLAIFER, R.O.
1967   *Analysis of Decisions under Uncertainty*, New York, NY: McGraw-Hill.

ULVILA, J.W.
1985   "Decision Trees for Forecasting", *Journal of Forecasting*, Vol. 4, 377-386.

6

REGRESSION ANALYSIS

*"I would not lead you into this promised land if I could, because if I could lead
you in, someone else could lead you out".*

E.V. Debs

6.1 RATIONALE

"The hypothesis is that we almost never face a random lack of knowledge. Ignorance, like knowledge, is purposefully directed".

Gunnar Myrdal

The main rationale of regression analysis as a forecasting method is that certain trends are primarily determined or explained by one or a few variables. This fact does not deny the complexity of the real world but rather questions the usefulness of explicitly taking into account all the complex factors. For example, if trends in international travel are highly determined by income, population, education, airline prices, marketing, and political stability, as well as several other variables, it is not unreasonable to predict the growth of international travel using only gross national product per capita. Indeed this variable has a positive impact on so many variables that "economic well-being" serves as a good proxy for many socio-economic variables. Often, it is better to use a simple model and a robust linear relationship, than to express reality using a host of complex variables. Complexity is no firm guarantee for accurate forecasts and often forecasters will strive to reduce the number of explanatory variables.

6.2 MODEL

"Reality is just too diverse and too complex to be handled in its entirety".

Anonymous

A model is the basis of regression analysis. As the quote says, reality is too complex to be handled in its entirety. The term 'model' in this context is used in its widest sense, and is not limited to complex relationships, but includes also the most simple forms of structures. Thus a model can be defined as simply a set of non-contradictory assumptions. Forecasting by using models implies the development of statistical relationships between the forecasted variable and a set of independent variables (or one variable). Such a relationship is sought in order to approximate as much as possible the "real" situation by way of establishing a "causality" among the two sides of the equation. This causality gave rise to the term "causal model" which expresses mathematically the relevant causal relationship between the dependent variable and one or more independent variables. Causal models are used when there is a priori good reason to believe that one or more variables are influenced or explained by another. Thus, the objective is to estimate or predict the "expected value" of one variable on the basis of observed values of another variable (or more) which, should have the following characteristics:

- be measurable and quantifiable;

- present some variations. For instance, weekly attendance at a ski resort cannot be explained by the weekly publicity budget if the amount of this budget is fixed on a weekly basis; and

- is reasonably independent from the forecasted variable.

Models are usually estimated by applying simple or multiple regression analysis which is one of the basic building blocks of many models. However, in using regression we must remember that all results are purely statistical in nature, i.e., they suggest a method of estimating the dependent variable without necessarily implying anything about the nature of the process which underlies the association found. There is nothing "regressive" or receding about regression analysis. The term is quite unfortunate and is due to a historical confusion based on Sir Francis Galton's (1822-1911) studies of inheritance in biology. He stated: "Each particularity in a man is shared by his Kinsman, but on the average, in a less degree (the law of universal regression)." He discovered that although tall fathers do tend to have tall sons, the average height of sons of a group of tall fathers is less than their father's height. Thus, Galton observed that the average height of the sons tended to "regress" toward the average height of the overall population of fathers, rather than toward reproducing the height of the parents.

In applying regression analysis, the forecaster is interested in the level some variables will assume in the future. Theoretically he/she knows that the level of the variable he/she wishes to forecast is "caused by" or is at least "associated with" the level of one or more variables. In some cases projection models are used. These models relate the forecasted variable to its past levels or to a time element. In other cases new variables are introduced. If only one explanatory variable is used, the model is bivariate and is often referred to as simple regression. In general, the use of regression analysis is based on four hypotheses, namely:

1) A statistical relationship is established between the forecasted variable and one or more independent or explanatory variables;

2) The parameters of this relationship are fairly stable if a variable is added or removed;

3) The explanatory variables can be selected among a large number of variables; and

4) Future values of the explanatory variables can be estimated.

6.3 LEAST-SQUARES METHOD

"The accumulation of reverse reaction products changes the reaction's predominant direction to the opposite".

Le Chatelier Principle

A young German mathematician named Gauss, estimating the orbits of the planets, concluded that the "best line" ought to represent the "most possible" values that could be inferred from the variable data. On the basis of this observation he developed the "Method of Least-

Squares" which states that the line of "best fit", the regression line, is the line that will minimize the sum of the squared vertical distances from each point to the line. Thus if

$$y = a + bx$$

is the line of "best fit", the vertical distances from each point to the line, if squared and added together, will result in a total that is less than that achieved by repeating the same process using any other line. A "vertical deviation" is the vertical distance from an observed point to the line. Each deviation in the sample is squared, and the least-squares line is defined to be the straight line that makes the sum of the square deviations a minimum. The regression line is found by estimating *(a)* and *(b)* (see below).

The basic model of a simple regression is:

$$\hat{y}_t = a + bx_t$$

where:

$\hat{y}$ = estimated value of y, the dependent variable

a = constant term

b = slope of the regression line $(\Delta y/\Delta x)$

x = the independent (explanatory) variable

t = the time subscript

The slope of the regression line, which is designated by the symbol *(b)*, is known as the "sample regression coefficient". It is the numerical value for the slope of the regression line, or the ratio of the change in the dependent variable (y) for every unit of change in the independent variable *(x)*. Thus, it is the ratio of the change in (y) divided by the change (Δ) in *(x)*, $(\Delta y/\Delta x)$, between any two points on the line. In this model, the relationship is linear, and the regression is the general equation of a straight line. The dependent variable (y) and the independent variable *(x)* are given, and the parameters *(a)* and *(b)* are to be estimated.

To illustrate the two-variable regression analysis, consider a simple "price-quantity" relationship: the level of sales of a computer game and its price (shown here in Table 6.1).

TABLE 6.1
PRICE-QUANTITY
DEMAND RELATIONSHIP

Year	Quantity Sold (thousands)	Price
1	10	900
2	15	800
3	20	750
4	26	700
5	33	680
6	40	650
7	48	620
8	56	600
9	70	575
10	82	550
11	100	510
12	120	499
13	150	480

Of course this demand relationship is quite naïve and in the real world it would probably not yield acceptable results. Several other factors play a role in determining the quantity sold. These factors might include:

- Quality,
- Publicity,
- Market penetration,
- Habit forming,

-       Competition,

-       etc...

Let us assume that the manufacturer of this computer game believes that business conditions will be reasonably similar in the future to what they are at present, and is prepared to forecast his future sales on the basis of the historical relationship between the price and the quantity sold. To obtain such a forecast the following steps are needed:

1)   Scatter Diagram

The first step in analyzing a time series is to plot the raw observations for all time periods, in terms of both the dependent and the explanatory variables. The characteristics of the trends (upward, downward, seasonality, stochastic behaviour, etc,...) will usually be visible. A scatter diagram is actually nothing more than a two-dimensional projection of a two-variable frequency distribution. It is the first attempt to discover the approximate form of the relationship by graphing it as points in the (x) , (y) plane. By means of it, one can quickly discern whether there is a relationship between (x) *and* (y) and whether this relationship may be linear or not.

The scatter diagram of the 13 points obtained from the data of Table 6.1 is shown in Figure 6.1.

FIGURE 6.1

SCATTER DIAGRAM

PRICE-QUANTITY RELATIONSHIP

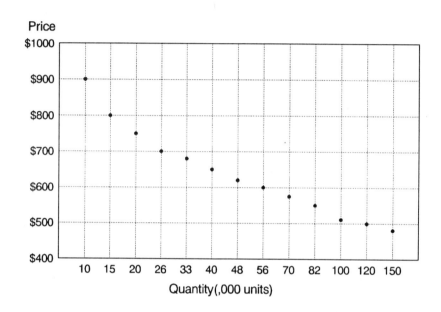

If there is no a priori reason for assuming linear association between two variables, an examination of the scatter diagram will permit one to make a fairly reliable judgment concerning the presence or absence of a linear association in a particular instance. An inspection of the above scatter diagram shows that its general trend is that of a straight line. The scatter plot not only "shows" the relationship between the two variables, but can also be used to indicate the type of equation which will better fit the existing data. If the data suggest a non-linear function then an appropriate equation will be applied (e.g. a curved line, a parabola, or an S-curve). While the scatter diagram is an advisable tool, it may not always be possible to establish the relationship between (*x*) *and* (*y*) by using a simple diagram.

2) Computation

The Least-Squares Method will be used to estimate *(a)* (vertical intercept) and *(b)* (slope of the regression line). When we state that:

$$y = f(x), \qquad \textit{y is a function of x}$$

and that this relationship between the two variables is linear and takes the following form:

$$y_t = a + bx_t$$

we simply acknowledge that the variable (x) does not take into account all the variations in (y). This equation captures only an "average" relationship. In no way does it preclude the possibility that, for given values of (x), actual realizations of (y) may depart markedly from this function. For this reason, as long as individual realizations are truly random, it is necessary to write the prediction equation derived from knowledge of the average relationship as a "true" relationship in the following way:

$$y_t = a + bx_t + \varepsilon$$

The quantity (y) is a linear function of the price (x) except for some error (ε) referred to as the stochastic term. Stochastic is a term derived from the Greek "Stokhos" meaning a target or a bull's eye and conveys a random scattering around a target. These errors are due to many causes which are not controlled or not identified in this simple model. They represent three possible situations:

- the net effect of excluded variables;
- the basic and unpredictable element of randomness in human behaviour; and/or

- the sum of the errors of observations or measurements of the variables in the model.

In practice, the stochastic or error term might be the result of all three reasons. Each error is believed to be small, and in their aggregate they cancel out:

$$\Sigma\varepsilon_i = 0$$

The objective of the Least-Squares Method is then to draw a line so that the sum of the squared value of these errors are as small as possible.

Thus:

$$min \ \Sigma \ \varepsilon_i^2 = \Sigma(y_i - \hat{y}_i)^2 = \Sigma(y_i - a - bx_i)^2$$

There are several ways to derive the constant (a) and the coefficient (b):

a = the (y) intercept

b = the slope of the regression line (the increase in value of y for every unit increase of x)

The slope of a line is defined by the vertical increase $(y_2 - y_1)$ divided by the horizontal increase $(x_2 - x_1)$ so that the slope b = $(y_2 - y_1) \ / \ (x_2 - x_1)$.

We will use:

$$a = \frac{(\Sigma y)(\Sigma x^2) - (\Sigma x)(\Sigma xy)}{n(\Sigma x^2) - (\Sigma x)^2}$$

as a general formula to calculate the estimated value of the intercept term (a). Applying this to the data in Table 6.1 yields:

$$a = \frac{(8,314)(68,054,000,000) - (770,000)(434,230,000)}{13(68,054,000,000) - (592,900,000,000)} = 793.15$$

The formula to calculate the estimator for the slope of the regression term is given by:

$$b = \frac{n(\Sigma xy) - (\Sigma x)(\Sigma y)}{n(\Sigma x^2) - (\Sigma x)^2}$$

Applying this formula to the same data results in:

$$b = \frac{13(434,230,000) - (770,000)(8,314)}{13(6,805,400,000) - (592,900,000,000)} = -0.0026$$

Computing the regression equation we obtain:

$$y = 793.15 - 0.0026\ x$$
$$(28.6) \quad (-6.8)$$
$$R^2 = 0.806 \quad D\text{-}W = 0.43$$

Thus, the "Least-Squares Method" which is also referred to as "Ordinary Least-Squares" (OLS) determines the value of the intercept (a) and the slope (b), so that the sum of the squared vertical deviations (residuals) between the data and the fitted line (residuals data fit), is less than the sum of the squared vertical deviations from any other straight line that could be fitted through the data. The vertical deviation is the vertical distance from an observed point to the line.

Total variation can be expressed in terms of:

- the variation explained by the regression is expressed by the vertical distance between any fitted (estimated) value and the mean or $(\hat{y}_i - \overline{y})$; and

- a residual portion called the unexplained variation, which is the vertical distance between the observed values and the estimated values $(y_i - \hat{y}_i)$.

Total variation is illustrated in Figure 6.2.

FIGURE 6.2
TOTAL VARIATION

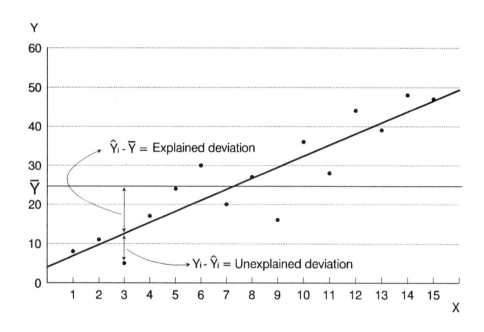

6.4 ASSUMPTIONS

"To be useful, a model need not be realistic in its every assumption. What matters is that it be realistic in its crucial ones".

Anonymous

The statistical power of the Least-Squares Regression model is built upon a series of assumptions often referred to as the assumptions of the classical linear model. These assumptions are listed below:

1)   Errors ε_i have a zero average:

$$E(y_i - \hat{y}_i) = E(\varepsilon_i) = 0 \quad for \ every \ i$$

For large number of observations on x, the average of ε_i is $= 0$

That is, the many influences that are combined in the error term are assumed to be unrelated to one another and to offset each other, so as to sum to zero in each time period.

2)   Homoscedasticity of the error terms:

For any set of $(x's)$ the variance of (y) shall be the same (i.e., constant variance). The dispersion of ε_i around the regression line is constant:

$$Var\ (\varepsilon_i)\ =\ \sigma^2_\varepsilon\ =\quad is\ constant\ for\ every\ \ x_i$$

(i.e. when (x) changes there is no new source of error which will modify the distribution of (ε_i)). If violated, we have heteroscedasticity of errors, or variation in dispersion of the error term. This situation might occur if the square of the error terms were greater in absolute size when the dependent variable (y) is large than when it is small. The converse, a large variance with small values of (y), would also be a departure.

Heteroscedasticity results in less precise estimates of the regression coefficient; that is, the estimates are subject to greater variability and are, thus, less certain. However, the estimates of (a) and (b) remain unbiased.

3) ε_i are independent,

(ε_i) and (ε_j) related to two distinct observations (i) and (j) are not correlated:

$$E\ (\varepsilon_i\ *\ \varepsilon_j)\ =\ 0\quad for\ every\ i \neq j$$

A departure from this assumption gives rise to the problem of autocorrelation, a systematic time pattern in the residuals. When autocorrelation is present, the usual tests of significance (Chapter 7) are not valid.

4)   Errors have a normal distribution of mean 0 and a variance (σ^2_ε) regardless of the values (x_i) of (x).

5)   The (x_i)'s are nonrandom variables whose values are fixed (i.e. nonstochastic).

6)   The random variables (y_i) are statistically independent. That is (y_2) is not affected by (y_i) or (y_3).

7) The relationship between (x_i) *and* (y_i) is linear.

8) No two independent variables should be identical. When two or more independent variables are highly correlated they are said to be collinear, and in this case multiple regression analysis gives inaccurate estimates of regression coefficients.

6.5 TREND PROJECTION

"It is our duty to proceed from what is near to what is distant, from what is known to that which is less known, to gather the traditions from those who have reported them, to correct them as much as possible and to leave the rest as it is, in order to make our work help anyone who seeks truth and loves wisdom".

Abu'l Rayhan Muhammad al-Biruni,
AD 973-1050

Trend projections are widely used since all they require is an accurate series of historical data. The technique assumes that the immediate future can be better predicted by the recent periods. Models of this type do not provide explanations as to the reasons backing this approach, or the "implicit" variables which are responsible for the trend. Trend analysis or extrapolation is not based on any theory; it is a "number's game". This may be due to the difficulty of developing a theory which can be applied to the numbers at hand, or it may simply be a concern about the cost of applying a complex model in relation to the benefits obtained by such a model. Thus no theory is introduced into the forecasting exercise. The interaction process is assumed to be marked by a high degree of continuity, and all the factors which influenced the trend in the past will continue to do so in the future. Trend projections are simple to apply since all they require is an accurate series of historical data. Random variations are smoothed by fitting a straight line to the data using the least-squares method of curve fitting. The line is then continued (extrapolated) into the future. The technique is based on the assumption that existing patterns will continue into the future - an assumption more likely to be correct over the short term than it is over the long term. For this reason trend projections provide reasonable forecasts for the immediate future but perform quite poorly further in the future, unless the data pattern is very stable. Most models of this type do not give any explicit guidance as to which past periods are relevant, how many to consider, or what importance to attach to the various periods. The simplest projection model can take the following form:

where:

$$\hat{y}_t = f(y_{t-1}) \; (actual \; value)$$

$\hat{y}$ = variable to be forecast

t = the subscript, refers to the period of time involved

To illustrate the method, consider the following example:

"The management of High Wave Swimming Pool is interested in forecasting future levels of attendance in order to estimate the budget requirement. Data on attendance is available for the past 14 years".

TABLE 6.2

ATTENDANCE AT HIGH WAVE POOL

Year	Attendance
1	30,000
2	28,000
3	34,000
4	38,000
5	41,000
6	40,000
7	46,000
8	50,000
9	52,000
10	55,000
11	61,000
12	67,000
13	72,000
14	76,000

Using the least-squares method to estimate the equation $\hat{y}_t = f(y_{t-1})$, we obtain:

$$Y_t = 599.546 + 1.0622Y_{t-1}$$
$$(15.1) \qquad (21.0)$$
$$R^2 = 0.974 \qquad D\text{-}W. = 1.0$$

A linear time-trend equation can also be used to project the level of attendance for any given year:

$$Y = a + bx$$

where:

$$Y = attendance$$

$$x = time \ (1,2,3,...14)$$

Time is used in trend projection as a "catch-all" variable. Estimating the above relationship by the Least-Squares Method we obtain:

$$Y = 22,087.91 + 3,626.374 \; x$$

Using this equation to forecast future levels of attendance can be done by substituting in the value of (x); here, year 15 and year 16 would take the values of (15) and (16) respectively.

$$Y_{15} = 22,087.91 + 3,626.374 \; (15)$$
$$= 76,483.52$$

$$Y_{16} = 22,087.91 + 3,626.374 \; (16)$$
$$= 80,109.89$$

A few remarks will be made to show the advantages and disadvantages of the Trend Projection Method:

i)   This method is based on the assumption that existing patterns will continue into the future. This assumption is more likely to be correct over the short term than it is over the long term, and for this reason this technique provides us with reasonably accurate forecasts for the immediate future but does quite poorly further into the future, unless the data patterns are very stable.

ii)   If a definite trend in the series being forecast exists, the above model will yield forecasts which are persistently too high or too low, depending on the direction of the trend.

iii)   To correct for the bias indicated in (ii) above, we can incorporate the trend into the projection model. One possibility is given in the following equation:

$$y_t = y_{t-1} + (y_{t-1} - y_{t-2})$$

This model adds the latest observed absolute period-to-period change to the most recent observed level of the variable. Applying this equation to the example of attendance at High Wave Pool (Table 6.2) we obtain the following estimates:

$$y_t = 2,571.94 + 1.048\ y_{t-1} + -0.262\ (y_{t-1} - y_{t-2})$$
$$(1.0) \qquad (18.1) \qquad\qquad (-0.9)$$
$$R^2 = 0.98 \qquad D\text{-}W. = 1.85$$

substituting the values of y_t in the above equation, yields estimates of attendance shown in Table 6.3.

TABLE 6.3
ESTIMATED ATTENDANCE
HIGH WAVE POOL

Year	Actual Attendance	Estimated Attendance
1	30,000	--
2	28,000	--
3	34,000	32,445
4	38,000	36,637
5	41,000	41,355
6	40,000	44,762
7	46,000	44,761
8	50,000	49,216
9	52,000	54,933
10	55,000	56,553
11	61,000	59,436
12	67,000	64,940
13	72,000	71,229
14	76,000	76,771

iv)   For some cases the rate of change may be of more interest than the absolute amount:

$$Y_t = y_{t-1} \left(\frac{y_{t-1}}{y_{t-2}} \right)$$

Note that this is not a regression equation. One can however treat the right hand side (RHS) as a single variable, add a constant and an error term, and estimate the equation as a linear regression.

Using the data from Table 6.2, the following estimates were obtained:

$$\text{Attendance} = 17217.56 + 0.6602 \text{ RHS}$$

$$(2.05) \qquad (4.39)$$

$$R^2 = 0.658 \qquad\qquad \text{D-W.} = 2.32$$

The actual versus the fitted values from this estimation are shown in Table 6.4.

TABLE 6.4

ESTIMATED ATTENDANCE

HIGH WAVE POOL, RATE OF CHANGE

Year	Estimated Attendance
1	--
2	--
3	34,472
4	33,157
5	57,847
6	46,334
7	47,651
8	40,041
9	62,993
10	54,241
11	52,870
12	58,347
13	68,317
14	69,730

6.5.1 EVALUATION

The technique assumes that the immediate future can be better predicted by the recent past periods. However it is fair to ask the following questions:

- *Which past periods are relevant?*
- *How many periods to consider?*
- *What importance should be attached to various periods?*

No general answers to the above questions can be determined a priori. However, a few "rules of thumb" may be applied, namely:

- the reliability of the forecast decreases with the number of years for which it is prepared;

- the time trend should be used as a "general" forecasting indicator;

- not to extend trend projections beyond the number of past years used for establishing the trend curve. In general, the projected period should not exceed half or one third of the existing time series; and

- the method should not be used when past growth has a logarithmic or exponential feature as in the case of "product diffusion" curves.

While the method is easy from a computational viewpoint it can still present a few difficulties such as:

- data collection and obtaining up-to-date data; and

- the possibility that management decisions may contribute to substantial variability in data such that past observations are of little use to the forecaster (e.g., special promotion campaign to attract new participants).

In general, trend projections have enjoyed widespread popularity because of their simplicity and low cost, even if no attempt is made to explain what is happening in the process. Instead, these types of projections rely exclusively on the principle of inertia through time. However, trends are not useless or absurd. The only absurdity is the extrapolation of the trend without relevance to variables which may alter this trend.

6.6 CAUSAL MODELS

"The budget equation of the mathematical economist applies also to himself: he purchases mathematical literacy with economic illiteracy. An economist after all is not an unemployed mathematician".

George Stigler

A Causal Model is usually based on a relationship between a dependent variable and one or more independent variables which are assumed to have an influence on the dependent variable. To illustrate an application of a "Causal Model" let us assume that Ice-O-Cream Ltd., which has a franchise to sell ice cream and soft drinks at the baseball stadium has observed that sales are positively affected by the level of temperature. To verify this hypothesis, data was collected for "sales" and "temperature" for the previous 15 games.

TABLE 6.5

SALES AND TEMPERATURE

BASEBALL STADIUM (ICE-O-CREAM LTD)

Game	Sales	Temperature (in F)
1	$2,020	70
2	1,810	65
3	2,600	77
4	1,940	69
5	1,710	64
6	2,006	69
7	2,300	75
8	2,200	76
9	2,600	78
10	2,100	72
11	1,800	70
12	2,250	74
13	2,400	78
14	2,700	80
15	2,080	73

A scatter diagram can be drawn using the 15 observations. This diagram will visually establish the relationship between the two variables.

FIGURE 6.3

SCATTER DIAGRAM
RELATIONSHIP BETWEEN ICE CREAM SALES
AND TEMPERATURE

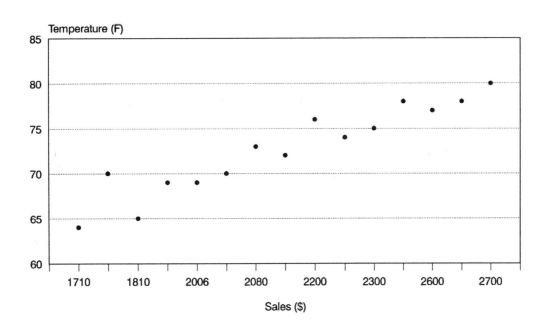

If we look at the extreme levels we obtain:

Expected sales of $1,710 when the temperature is 64

Expected sales of $2,700 when the temperature is 80

Thus, the change in expected sales per degree change in temperature is:

$$\frac{\$2,700 - \$1,710}{80° - 64°} = \frac{990}{16} = 61.88$$

This relationship between sales and temperature can be expressed as a mathematical equation:

Ice cream sales = 1,710 + 61.88 (temperature – 64)

Thus, if the temperature is 73 , ice cream sales are expected to be:

1,710 + 61.88 (73 – 64) =

1,710 + 61.88 (9) =

1,710 + 556.92 = $2,266.92

By using past data, the relationship between ice cream sales and temperature can be quantified, and the significance of the complete model as a prediction device can be ascertained. The relationship can be estimated by the standard regression equation:

$$Y = a + bx$$

where:

$$Y = \text{ice cream sales}$$
$$x = \text{temperature}$$

Estimating this equation by the Least-Squares Method yields the following results:

$$Y = -2,186.57 + 59.92 \; x$$

Using this regression equation, it is possible to predict sales of ice cream given the temperature of a particular day. If the temperature is 73 , then sales are expected to be:

Sales = -2,186.57 + 59.92 (73) = $2,187.59

The "causal" model may contain more than one "independent" variable. It seems reasonable to assume that sales of ice cream at baseball games would depend on the "attendance" at the baseball games. If we were provided with the attendance figures for each game, we could state a multiple regression equation such as:

$$Y = a + b_1 x_1 + b_2 x_2$$

where:

Y = ice cream sales

x_1 = temperature

x_2 = attendance at each game

Using available data for the 15 games shown in Table 6.6, a multiple regression equation to estimate ice cream sales was computed yielding the following results:

$$y = 1005.18 + 26.61 x_1 + 0.077 x_2$$
$$(-1.7) \qquad (2.0) \qquad (2.7)$$
$$R^2 = 0.924$$

TABLE 6.6

SALES, TEMPERATURE AND ATTENDANCE

BASEBALL STADIUM

Game	Sales	Temperature	Attendance
1	$2,020	70	15,620
2	1,810	65	13,400
3	2,600	77	17,810
4	1,940	69	14,000
5	1,710	64	12,050
6	2,006	69	15,500
7	2,300	75	16,708
8	2,200	76	15,930
9	2,600	78	18,450
10	2,100	72	16,380
11	1,800	70	13,020
12	2,250	74	16,200
13	2,400	78	18,700
14	2,700	80	20,100
15	2,080	73	16,500

It should be noted that the causal model in itself is not a guarantee for a good forecast, and the logic of the proposed relationship should be considered carefully in the choice of the independent variables.

The use of causal models for forecasting depends essentially on the following three assumptions:

- The appropriate independent variables can be selected from among the infinitely large number of possible variables;

- The relationship between the independent variables and the dependent variable will change at some predetermined rate; and

- Accurate predictions of the future values of the causal factors can be established.

Prediction from a regression relation is only valid provided the population samples are not expected to change, in any relevant respect, between the estimation of the regression and its application to prediction. Further, projections are only as good as the predictions for the future values of the independent variables. Offsetting this is the advantage that, if predictions of causal factors are adequate, the net effect of each change in each factor may be established independently, thus permitting examination of the relationship in detail. It should be recognized that the model is likely to be revised across time as experience is gained and relationships change.

A useful function of causal models is that changes in the value of the independent variables can easily be incorporated in the model and the impact of these on the dependent variable measured. For instance, consider the following relationship:

Attendance at a ski resort = f [publicity budget ($) and the amount of snowfall (inches)]

While management is hopeless about climate conditions and its influence on attendance, the publicity budget can be easily controlled, and its influence on attendance measured. This is illustrated in the following case of attendance at a ski resort (Table 6.7). Applying the Least-Squares Method, the above relationship was estimated yielding the following results:

$$y = 1.318 + 0.292 \, x_1 + 0.0014 \, x_2$$
$$(6.7) \quad (0.01)$$
$$R^2 = 0.909$$

where:

y = attendance

x_1 = publicity budget

x_2 = snowfall

TABLE 6.7

ATTENDANCE AT MOUNTAIN PEAK SKI RESORT

Season	Attendance (thousands)	Snowfall (inches)	Publicity Budget (thousands $)
1	12	120	40
2	14	110	60
3	16	126	61
4	13	110	40
5	10	100	38
6	18	131	70
7	21	128	85
8	24	125	90
9	22	122	92
10	30	126	100
11	28	127	90
12	34	128	110

6.7 TIME SERIES ANALYSIS

"La connaissance du futur doit resulter essentiellement d'un acte d'imagination; rien du futur ne peut être déduit du présent".

P. Massé

Time Series Analysis is more complex than the "simple trend projection". While both techniques rely on past historical data, they differ in the degree of complexity of the treatment of the data. Trend projection for a future period is on the basis of "past trends" or the behaviour of previous periods. In the case of Time Series Analysis the computation is often more intricate and there is an "explanatory objective" in the data manipulation. Indeed time series analysis helps to identify and explain:

- Any regularity or systematic variation in the series of data which is due to seasonality;
- Cyclical patterns that repeat any two or three years or more;
- Trends in the data; and/or
- Growth rates of these trends.

The main assumption of a time series model is that the pattern will recur over time. Obviously this assumption is more likely to be valid in the short term and for relatively stable data. Thus Time Series Analysis is likely to be most appropriate in short-term forecasting and where there is a relatively stable variable being forecast. In the longer term, major socio-economic variables, participation rates, consumer tastes, demographic distribution and societal values can change and render historical patterns very unstable for forecasting purposes.

In this section three methods will be reviewed:

1) Moving Average;
2) Weighted Moving Average; and
3) Exponential Smoothing.

6.7.1 MOVING AVERAGE METHOD

"It was too bad that so intelligent a man had made such a fatal error in judgement so late in life".

Mario Puzo, The Godfather

The simplest type of time series forecast is to use the last value as the forecast for the next period. However, the previous month is data may have been heavily influenced by random fluctuations, making the forecast very inaccurate. One method to reduce the influence of strong random fluctuations is to compute a moving average of several months hoping that the positive and negative random elements will tend to "average out". Essentially, the Moving Average Method is applicable when the data are fluctuating in the short run while maintaining a basic tendency in the long run. Dealing with such a statistical series, the forecaster would be interested to "level off" the short run variations in order to highlight the main trend which will then serve as a basis for the forecaster. The Moving Average Method will "smooth" the fluctuating data by replacing each observation by an arithematic average. The method is described notationally as:

$$ F_{t+1} = \frac{Y_t + Y_{t-1} + Y_{t-2} + ... + Y_{t-n+1}}{n} $$

$$ = \frac{1}{n} \sum_{i=t-n+1}^{t} Y_t $$

where:

F_t = forecast for the period t, so F_{t+1} is the forecast for the next period, $_{t+1}$

Y_t = the observation at period t

n = the number of observations used in the average.

Table 6.8 shows the monthly attendance figures at Surefun Fitness Club along with the forecast produced by the moving average technique.

TABLE 6.8
FORECASTING BY MOVING AVERAGES
SUREFUN FITNESS CLUB

Period	Attendance	Three-month Moving Average	Error %
1	1,200		
2	1,100		
3	1,050		
4	1,070	1,117	4.4
5	1,095	1,073	2.3
6	1,150	1,072	6.8
7	1,230	1,105	10.2
8	1,310	1,158	11.6
9	1,200	1,230	2.5
10	1,100	1,247	13.4
11	1,050	1,203	14.6
12	1,020	1,117	9.5

By using a 3-month moving average, a forecast for period 4 is calculated as follows:

$$1/3 \ (Y_1 + Y_2 + Y_3) = \frac{1,200 + 1,100 + 1,050}{3} = 1,117$$

The same process is applied to obtain subsequent monthly forecasts. The forecasting error is computed by comparing actual and forecasted values:

$$Forecasting \ error = \frac{1,117 - 1,070}{1,070} \ x \ 100 = 4.4\%$$

The average forecasting error is 8.3 percent and the method used yielded forecasts only one period ahead, that is, the values for periods 1, 2 and 3 are used to forecast period 4. If it is absolutely necessary to forecast several periods, the forecast can be treated as "real values" and used to forecast subsequent periods. However, this approach is not satisfactory and the reliability of the forecast is questionable.

As an example, assume we want to forecast period 14. Then:

$$\hat{Y}_{14} = \frac{\hat{Y}_{13} + Y_{12} + Y_{11}}{3}$$

$$= \frac{\hat{Y}_{13} + 1,020 + 1,050}{3}$$

Because $\hat{Y}_{13}$ is unavailable, an intermediate step is required. The best estimate for this period is the moving average for period 13:

$$\hat{Y}_{13} = \frac{Y_{12} + Y_{11} + Y_{10}}{3}$$

$$= \frac{1,020 + 1,050 + 1,100}{3} = 1,057$$

By substituting its value we obtain:

$$\hat{Y}_{14} = \frac{1,057 + 1,020 + 1,050}{3} = 1,042$$

6.7.2 WEIGHTED MOVING AVERAGE

"The actual building of roads devoted to motor cars is not for the near future, in spite of many rumors to that effect".

Harpers Weekly, 1902

In the Weighted Moving Average method the limitation of equal weights can be corrected by assigning weights to the data based on their proximity to the current period. The data for each period are multiplied by a weight, with the weights declining as the observations recede into the past. The weighted observations are then divided by the sum of the weights. The weights could be numbers such as: 3, 2 and 1; assigned to periods Y_t, Y_{t-1}, and Y_{t-2} or decimals (0.5, 0.4 and 0.3); or fractions ($\frac{1}{2}$, $\frac{1}{4}$ and $\frac{1}{8}$). The specification of the weights to be used is decided largely by the level of accuracy of the technique on prior data.

Using data from Table 6.8, a weighted scheme can be adopted where the most recent observation would be given a weight of 50%, the next most recent observation given a weight of 30%, and the third observation a weight of 20%. The forecast would be determined as follows:

50% of 1,050 = 525

30% of 1,100 = 330

20% of 1,200 = <u>240</u>

1,095

Since the weighted moving average discounts the value of past observations, it tends to be more responsive to the genuine changes in "attendance". However, in using a weighted moving average, the problems involved in selecting the appropriate number of periods for a moving average become compounded. One now has to search for the combination of periods and weights which minimize the forecast error.

6.7.3 EXPONENTIAL SMOOTHING

"Exponential smoothing is a very elegant term for what is inherently a highly commonsense-oriented idea".

Thomas E. Vollmann

The logic underlying exponential smoothing is that each observation reveals more information about the time series in question and therefore should be immediately incorporated into the values of the model coefficient. Moreover, recent observations are more important than older ones for forecasting the immediate future, thus a weighting scheme is used where the smoothing assigns the greatest weight to more recent observations and exponentially decreases these weights to older observations.

The Moving Average Method assigns the weight to all the (n) observations and none to the observations prior to (t-n). That is, the weight given to the latest observations (n) is (1/n), and zero to all previous observations. It can be argued that, for forecasting purposes, while recent observations have probably a higher impact than older observations, the latter should be taken into consideration in one form or another. While the weighted moving average represents an improvement over the simple moving average method, it somehow lacks mathematical rigor, the weights are often assigned on a pragmatic basis without the backing of a valid rationale and it does not react to changes in the data. For these reasons the method of exponential smoothing is introduced. The method systematically revises the estimates of the coefficients of a forecasting model based on each successive actual observation. It has an appeal among forecasters because of the logic:

"If the forecast for a particular period was too high, reduce it for the next period, if it was too low, raise it".

The basic formula for computing the single-exponential-smoothing statistic is:

$$F_{t+1} = \propto Y_t + (1 - \propto) [\propto Y_{t-1} + \propto (1 - \propto) Y_{t-2} + \propto (1 - \propto)^2 Y_{t-3}...]$$

and F_t (being the same as the expression appearing in the squared brackets) one can re-write (F_{t+1}) as :

$$F_{t+1} = \propto Y_t + (1 - \propto) F_t$$

and the exponentially smoothed forecast for period (t + 1) is ($\propto$) times the actual value for (t) plus (1 - $\propto$) times the exponentially smoothed weighted average for (t). This can also be expressed as :

$$F_{t+1} = F_t + \propto (Y_t - F_t)$$

Thus the new forecast (T_{t+1}) = old forecast (F_t) + $\propto$ times the error in the old forecast. Or the new estimates = old estimates + "fraction" of error.

The error = actual value – forecasted value

The fraction must be between 0 and 1, and is termed "the exponential smoothing constant" ($\propto$). This means that the sum of the weights add up to one, as illustrated by the following example :

If $\propto = 0.3$, then the weights are :

$$0.3 + 0.3 (1 - 0.3) + 0.3 (1 - 0.3)^2 + 0.3 (1 - 0.3)^3 + ...$$
$$= 0.3 + 0.21 + 0.147 + 0.1029 + ...$$

This series approaches a total value of 1. It should be noted that the closer $\propto$ is to 1, the greater the new forecast will incorporate an adjustment for the error in the immediately prior forecast; and the greater the weight given to the most recent period. The nearer $\propto$ is to 0, the less sensitive the new forecast will be to the error in the immediately prior forecast. $(1 - \propto)$ is the weight given to preceding periods in calculating the forecast. If the smoothing constant $(\propto)$ equals 0.3, the weights shown in Table 6.9 are given to the preceding periods.

TABLE 6.9
THE SMOOTHING CONSTANT

Time Period	Calculation	Weight
t		0.3
t-1	0.7 x 0.3	0.21
t-2	0.7 x 0.7 x 0.3	0.147
t-3	0.7 x 0.7 x 0.7 x 0.3	0.103
t-4	0.7 x 0.7 x 0.7 x 0.7 x 0.3	0.072
All others		0.168
Total		**1.00**

For greater responsiveness to forecast errors, the smoothing constant value may be increased. However, too high of a value (or values) may cause over-reaction to forecast errors. An important step in making an exponentially smoothed forecast is the selection of the value. The most commonly used values range from 0.10 to 0.25. The usual method of selecting an $(\propto)$ value is to try several different levels of $(\propto)$ to "forecast" known values of recent periods. The $(\propto)$ level that gives the best forecast is then used for forecasting future period values. Due to the heavier weighting of recent observations, the accuracy of this type of forecast is generally better than a moving average forecast.

One way of selecting $(\propto)$ is to simulate the historical data using alternative values of $(\propto)$. The value of $(\propto)$ that yields the best forecasts thus becomes the appropriate smoothing constant. However this method is time-consuming and costly, and can be substituted by selecting a value of ($\propto$) related to the data pattern. If the data reveals little random variation, ($\propto$) should be relatively small. Alternatively, if there are larger fluctuations in the data, ($\propto$) should be large. The smoothing constant ($\propto$) can also be approximated by the following relationship:

$$\propto \ = \ \frac{2}{n \ + \ 1}$$

Thus:

TABLE 6.10
RELATIONSHIP BETWEEN THE SMOOTHING CONSTANT AND THE NUMBER OF OBSERVATIONS

Number of observations n	Value of $\propto$
19	0.100
15	0.125
12	0.154
9	0.200
6	0.286
4	0.400
3	0.500

To illustrate the method, consider the following:

"A sports shop estimates to sell 50 pairs of skis of a particular brand in a particular week. The store manager held a reserve of an additional 25 pairs to meet unexpected demand. During the week, 60 pairs were sold. If the smoothing constant is 0.3, what is next week's forecast?".

Next week's forecast = 50 + 0.3 (60 - 50) = 53 pairs.

Since the initial forecast was low, the exponential smoothing raised its value. If the situation had been the reverse, that is, a forecast of 60 but only 50 units demanded, the result would be :

Next week's forecast = 60 + 0.3 (50 - 60) = 57 pairs.

Using data from Table 6.8 a forecast is produced by exponential smoothing using three different levels of (∞) :

TABLE 6.11
FORECASTING BY EXPONENTIAL SMOOTHING

Period	Attendance	∞ = 0.10	∞ = 0.30	∞ = 0.50
1	1,200	1,111	1,111	1,111
2	1,100	1,120	1,138	1,155
3	1,050	1,118	1,126	1,128
4	1,070	1,110	1,103	1,089
5	1,095	1,107	1,094	1,079
6	1,150	1,106	1,094	1,087
7	1,230	1,110	1,111	1,118
8	1,310	1,122	1,147	1,174
9	1,200	1,141	1,196	1,242
10	1,100	1,147	1,197	1,221
11	1,050	1,142	1,168	1,160
12	1,020	1,133	1,132	1,105

6.7.4 EVALUATION

While the moving average forecasting technique is one of the easiest time series models, it has few major limitations:

i)   longer-term forecasts tend to lose accuracy rapidly;

ii)   the moving average never forecasts turning points;

iii)   a moving average is influenced only by those periods included in the average. Any observations prior to period t-n+1 are ignored altogether in the forecast; and

iv)   each period shares equally in the forecast. It could be argued that more recent observations have a greater influence on the forecast and should be given different weights. This can be corrected by the weighted moving average method.

Because of the heavier weighting of the recent observations, the accuracy of exponentially smoothed forecasts is generally somewhat better than that of moving average forecasts. However, the method is solely based on the assumption that patterns observed in the past will continue in the future. This might not be true and changing future events may invalidate the forecasts. All in all, the technique has three major limitations :

1)   The model must be updated each time a new data point becomes available. This update is useful in regression analysis, but it is critical in the case of exponential-smoothing;

2)   The accuracy of the prediction of the method is highly limited by one or two periods in the future; and

3) The subjective determination of the appropriate value of the weights may affect the results of the forecasts.

6.8 STUDY QUESTIONS

1) Why do we use a "model" to represent reality?

2) In your own words, define the concept of a "model". Provide an example.

3) Which characteristics should the "predictor" variable possess?

4) Name the four hypothesis upon which the use of regression analysis is based.

5) What is the difference between y and ŷ?

6) Construct a "Scatter Diagram" using the following data representing a relationship between "hours of practise" and "score" of basketball players during a season.

TABLE 6.12

PERFORMANCE OF BASKETBALL PLAYERS

Score	Hours of Practice
150	300
162	310
103	240
100	220
75	170
104	200
64	120
40	80
85	150
90	160

7)   Using data in Table 6.12, estimate the following relationship using the Least-Squares Method:

$$y = a + bx$$

where:

    y = score of players

    x = hours of practice

8)   In which situations is it useful to lag the independent variable? Provide an example.

9)   Identify other possible independent variables in the relationship shown in Question 7.

10)   Apply the "Moving Average Method" to the following data of monthly sales of ski equipment (use a 2-month moving average).

TABLE 6.13

SALES OF SKI EQUIPMENT

Period	Sales (thousands $)
1	14
2	16
3	10
4	9
5	8
6	7
7	7
8	12
9	13
10	18
11	19
12	14

11)   Repeat the same forecast (Table 6.13) using a 3-month moving average.

12)   Which moving average yields a better forecast, the 2-month or the 3-months Why?

13)   Use the results obtained in answering Questions 10 and 11 to estimate the values of periods 13 and 14.

6.9 BIBLIOGRAPHY

AMEEN, J.R. and P.J. HARRISON
1984 "Discount Weighted Estimation", *Journal of Forecasting*, Vol. 3, 285-296.

ARCHER, B.H.
1987 Demand Forecasting and Estimation, Ch 7 of Ritchie J.R.B., and Goeldner, C.R. (eds.), *Travel, Tourism and Hospitality Research*, New York: John Wiley, 77-86.

BEAMAN, J.
1976 Statistical Projections That go Beyond Projections of Past Trends, *Canadian Outdoor Recreation Demand Study Technical Note 13*, Toronto, ON: Ontario Research Council on Leisure.

BOWERMAN, B.L. and R.T. O'CONNELL
1979 *Time Series and Forecasting*, North Scituate, MA: Duxbury Press.

BOX, G.E.P. and G.M. JENKINS
1976 *Time Series Analysis*, San Francisco: Holden-Day.

BROWN, W.G. and F. NAWAS
1973 Impact of Aggregation on the Estimation of Outdoor Recreation Demand Functions, *American Journal of Agriculture Economics*, 55, 246-249.

CARMAN, R.L.
1990 The Pitfalls and Profits of Time Series Analysis, *Leisure Studies*, Andover, Eng., 9 (3), 259-266.

COELEN, S.P.
1980 "Regression Analysis of Regional Quality of Life", *Social Indicators Research*, Vol. 8 (4), 467-479.

COOPERSMITH, L.W.
1983 "Forecasting Time Series Which are Inherently Discontinuous", *Journal of Forecasting*, Vol. 2 (3), 225-235.

ELSNER, G.H.
1971 "A Regression Method for Estimating The Level of Use and Market Area of a Proposed Large Ski Resort", *Journal of Leisure Research*, Vol. 3, 160-167.

FESSENMAIER, D.R., M.F. GOODCHILD and LIEBER, S.R.
1980   Correlates of Day Hiking Participation: The Effects of Aggregation, *Journal of Leisure Research*, 12, 213-228.

FISHER, M.J.
1988   The Twenty-first Century: A Prognosticator's View of Futuristic Trends in Health, Physical Education and Recreation, In Carre, F.A. (ed.), *I.C.P.E.R./C.A.H.P.E.R. World Conference: Towards the 21st Century*, Vancouver, BC: University of British Columbia, 204-210.

GARDNER, E.S. Jr.
1985   "Exponential Smoothing: The State of the Arts", *Journal of Forecasting*, Vol. 4, 1-28.

GORDON, T.J.
1991   "Notes on Forecasting and Chaotic Series Using Regression", *Technological Forecasting and Social Change*, Vol. 39 (3), 337-348.

HOF, J.G. and H.F. KAISER
1983   "Long-term Outdoor Recreation Participation Projections for Public Land Management Agencies", *Journal of Leisure Research*, Vol. 15, 1-14.

INTRILIGATOR, M.D.
1978   *Econometric Models, Techniques and Applications*, Englewood Cliffs, NJ: Prentice-Hall.

JENKINS, G.J.
1979   *Practical Experiences with Modelling and Forecasting Time Series*, St. Helier: Jenkins and Partners.

LATHAM, J.
1990   Statistical Trends in Tourism and Hotel Accommodation, in C.P. Cooper (ed.), *Progress in Tourism, Recreation, and Hospitality Management: Volume 2*, London: Bellhaven, 117-128.

LEVINE, R.L. and J.E. HUNTER
1983   "Regression Methodology: Correlation, Meta-Analysis, Confidence Intervals and Reliability", *Journal of Leisure Research*, Vol. 15, 323-343.

LUPTON, C.H., et al.
1984   Participation in Leisure-Time Physical Activity: A Comparison of Existing Data, *Journal of Physical Education, Recreation, & Dance*, 55 (9), 19-23.

MAKRIDAKIS, S., A. ANDERSON, R. CARBONE, R. FILDES, M. HIBON,
R. LEWANDOWSKI, J. NEWTON, E. PARZEN and R. WINKLER
1982   "The Accuracy of Extrapolation (Times Series) Methods: Results of a Forecasting
       Competition", *Journal of Forecasting*, Vol. 1, 111-154.

MAKRIDAKIS, S. and S.C. WHEELWRIGHT
1978   *Forecasting Methods and Applications*, New York, NY: John Wiley and Sons.

MCDORWALL, D., R. McCLEARN and E.E. MEIDINGER
1980   *Interrupted Time Series Analysis*, Beverly Hills, CA: Sage Publications.

MONTGOMERY, D.C. and L.A. JOHNSON
1976   *Forecasting and Time Series Analysis*, New York, NY: McGraw-Hill Book Co.

MOSTELLER, F. and J.W. TUKEY
1977   *Data Analysis and Regression*, Reading, MA: Addison-Wesley Publishing Co.

NEWBOLD, P.
1983   "ARIMA Model Building and the Time Series Analysis Approach to Forecasting",
       Journal of Forecasting, Vol. 2, 23-36.

NG, D.
1984   A Model: Estimating the Demand for Leisure Services Manpower: Forecasting with
       Multiple Regression, the Subjective/Objective Qualitative Forecasting, and the Delphi
       Methodology, *World Leisure and Recreation*, 26 (5), 45-49.

OLIVEIRA, R.A., L.M. ARTHUR and A.C. PAPASTAVROU
1983   "A Distributed Lag Approach to Forecasting Wilderness Use", *Journal of Leisure
       Research*, Vol. 15, 52-64.

OSTROM, C.W.
1978   *Time Series Analysis: Regression Techniques*, Beverly Hills, CA: Sage Publications.

SCARDINO, V.A., J. SCHWALBE and M. BEAUREGARD
1980   Forecasting Trends in Outdoor Recreation Activities on a Multi-State Basis, In *1980
       National Outdoor Recreation Trend Symposium Broomal, Pa.*, Durham, NH: National
       Outdoor Recreation Trends Symposium.

SCHROEDER, T.D.
1983   "Use of Multiple Regression in Recreation Research: A Discussion of Several Issues",
       Journal of Leisure Research, Vol. 15, 247-250.

SMITH, V.K.
1975   The Estimation and Use of Models of the Demand for Outdoor Recreation, In *Assessing*

the Demand for Outdoor Recreation Appendix B. Washington, DC: USDI, Bureau of Outdoor Recreation.

SPECHT, D.A.
1975   "On the Evaluation of Causal Models", *Social Science Research*, Vol. 4 (2), 113-133.

STEINNES, D.N. and R.L. RAAB
1983   A Time Series Approach to Forecasting Angling Activity at a Recreational Site Based on Past Success, *Canadian Journal of Fisheries and Aquatic Sciences*, 40 (12), 2189-2193.

STYNES, D.J.
1983   An Introduction to Recreation Forecasting, In Lieber, S.R. and D.R. Fesenmaier (eds.), *Recreation Planning and Management*, State College, PA: Venture Publishing Inc., 87-95.

STYNES, D.J.
1983   Time Series and Structural Models for Forecasting Recreation, In Lieber, S.R. and D.R. Fesenmaier (eds.), *Recreation Planning and Management*, State College, PA: Venture Publishing Inc., 105-119.

SWAMY, P.A.V.B. and G.J. SCHINASI
1989   "Should Fixed Coefficients be Re-estimated every Period for Extrapolation?", *Journal of Forecasting*, Vol. 8, 1-18.

VANREUSEL, B.
1987   A Time Trend Analysis of Sport Participation Styles, In *Physical Culture and Sports in the Way of Life of the Young Generation*, Prague: International Committee for Sociology of Sport, 307-331.

WEIGHTMAN, G.
1978   "The Tricky Game of Population Trends", *New Society*, Vol. 43, 363-365.

WHEELWRIGHT, S.C. and S. MAKRIDAKIS
1980   *Forecasting Methods for Management*, 3rd ed. New York, NY: John Wiley and Sons.

WILKINSON, P.F.
1973   "The Use of Models in Predicting the Consumption of Outdoor Recreation", *Journal of Leisure Research*, Vol. 5, 34-48.

7

MEASURES OF RELIABILITY

"Behind Moses striking the rock is the whole Israel; behind the sorcerer following his divining rod is the anxiety of a whole village wanting to obtain new water supplies; and behind the forecaster's predictions is a society confusing wishes with reality".

Anonymous

7.1 CORRELATION COEFFICIENT

To measure the "goodness of fit" of the regression line, the correlation coefficient (R) is calculated. Using data from Table 6.1, (R) is obtained by applying the following formula:

$$R = \frac{N\Sigma xy - (\Sigma x)(\Sigma y)}{\sqrt{[N\Sigma x^2 - (\Sigma x)^2][N\Sigma y^2 - (\Sigma y)^2]}}$$

$$R = \frac{13(434,230,000) - (770,000)(8,314)}{\sqrt{[13(5,504,426) - (69,129,596)][13(68,054,000,000 - 592,900,000,000)}}$$

R= -0.8978

The correlation coefficient can vary from a value of +1 to −1. It should be noted that a negative correlation coefficient indicates as close a degree of linear association as does a positive correlation coefficient of the same absolute value. When there is no linear association between the sample variables, (R) is 0; when the linear association in the sample is perfect, it is +1 or −1.

A quick way to estimate the correlation coefficient involves the use of quadrants. This is done by applying the following steps:

i)   Calculate the arithmetic mean of (y) and (x);

ii)   Build a diagram and show (y, x) as well as all the observed values in the four quadrants. The quadrants reflect the arithmetic means of (y and x).

FIGURE 7.1
GRAPHICAL METHOD
CORRELATION COEFFICIENT

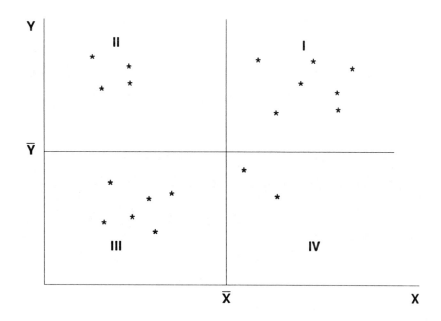

iii) Calculate the number of observations in each quadrant. For the points in I and III quadrants, the products of the deviations from the origin are positive, and for the points in II and IV quadrants they are negative. For the above example we have:

II and IV	=	– 6 points
I and III	=	+ 13 points
Difference	+	7 points

iv)   *Estimated R* = $+ \dfrac{7}{19} = 0.368$

The coefficient of correlation should not be interpreted as a measure of "cause and effect" relationship but only as something that measures the degree of association among variables. It does not establish causality, and as such, does not identify one variable as independent and the other as dependent. Causal relationships can only be determined by specific knowledge exogenous to the statistical manipulation. In the areas of sports and recreation this knowledge will be based on:

- *social relationships such as: friends, family, and work environment;*
- *psychological relationships such as: motivations, satisfaction, and personality types;*
- *political relationships such as: subsidies, and priorities;*
- *marketing relationships such as: publicity and its effect on demand; and/or*
- *economic relationships such as: price, elasticities, and consumer preferences.*

Situations such as the following may occur:

1) **Spurious Correlation**

All statistical analysis can capture is correlation; it cannot capture causality. Over a given period of time, it is possible for any two data series to move together for any number of reasons. This is what forecasters refer to as "spurious correlation". The correlation may be due to chance. For example: suppose that over a certain period of time the number of joggers has increased and that, over the same period, sales of summer cottages also showed a gain. Then, if the following relationship is tested:

Cottage sales = f (number of joggers),

it would probably show a high correlation coefficient which is not founded on any theoretical grounds, but only on the fact that both variables had reasonably similar variations over a certain period. Regression analysis is often misused as a tool to "explain" or "establish a relationship" between two sets of variables.

2) Covariation Effect

For instance, sales of cars could be correlated with sales of sports equipment. No real relationship can be established between these two variables. However, both are probably affected by economic conditions.

3) Causation Effect

This is the case where regression analysis has a useful function to fulfil. It is therefore essential to establish, a priori, a meaningful relationship between the two variables, in order to avoid obtaining statistically valid results but without any theoretical foundations. The variable that is supposed to be the cause of the variations in the other is usually taken as the independent or explanatory variable. However, in some situations there is confusion between the cause and the effect.

4) Reliability

To check for the reliability of the coefficient of correlation, one has to refer to tabular values provided in Appendix A. To use the table effectively, the correct "degrees of freedom" must be entered. This is always the number of observations minus the number of variables. For example, if n = 12 and k = 2 (*y and x*), we have:

$$Degrees\ of\ freedom\ (df) = n - k = 12 - 2 = 10$$

In the table (Appendix A) we find $r_{.05,10} = .576$ ($r = R$). If the calculated (R) exceeds these values, then the coefficient of correlation is reliable at the 5 percent level. Higher levels of reliability can also be calculated (e.g. for reliability at the 1% level, $r_{.01,10} = .708$).

If the derived value of (R) which we want to evaluate is equal to .860, then this value must meet or exceed the tabular value for the 5 percent level to be considered as reliable. In this case we reject the null hypothesis and accept the alternative hypothesis that the true correlation value represented by our sample correlation value is not zero, and that our estimate of the correlation coefficient is reliable. If the value of (r) is not reliable at the 5 percent level, we would be forced to assume that there was not a reliable relationship between the dependent (y) variable and the independent (x) variable.

We can generate our own tabular values using the t-ratio table:

$$r = \sqrt{\frac{t^2}{t^2 + n - K}}$$

example: $r_{.01,10}$ $= 0.708$

Obtained from: $t_{.01,10}$ $= 3.17$

Substituting for n = 10, k = 2, t = 3.17:

$$r_{.01,10} = \sqrt{\frac{(3.17)^2}{(3.17)^2 + (12-2)}} = .708$$

This process could turn out to be handy if it were useful to set (R) at some level other than 5% or 1% (the limits imposed by the table).

7.2 COEFFICIENT OF DETERMINATION

The coefficient of determination is the percentage of the total variation in the dependent (y) variable that can be accounted for by the linear relationship between the independent and the dependent variable (x and y).

$$\text{Coefficient of determination} = R^2 \times 100$$

It provides a good measure of the importance of (R) relative to prediction. It can also be expressed as the amount of total variance in the dependent variable "explained" by the independent variable in the equation, over that which could be explained by the mean of dependent variable alone. Thus, (R^2) measures the extent to which movements in the dependent variable are being explained by the estimated model:

$$R^2 = \frac{\sum\limits_{t=1}^{n} (\hat{Y}_t - \bar{Y})^2}{\sum\limits_{t=1}^{n} (Y_t - \bar{Y})^2}$$

$$R^2 = \frac{\textit{Variation explained by the equation}}{\textit{Total variation of the dependent variable}}$$

This indicates why the correlation coefficient squared works as a measure of the strength of a relationship. If ($R^2 = 1$), then:

explained variation = total variation

and,

unexplained variation = 0

If the unexplained variation is equal to zero then the sum of all the residuals is zero and therefore all the residuals must individually be equal to zero. The points must all lie exactly on the line. ($R^2 = 1$) thus signifies perfect correlation. If ($R^2 = 0$) then:

unexplained variation = total variation

Important points are:

- (R^2) takes on values ranging from a low of zero (0) to a high of one (1);
- the higher the (R^2) the more variability is being explained;

. (R^2) can be used for comparing the relative performance of two models when the dependent variables are the same. For example, if we have the following two alternative models:

$$y = f(x_1) \quad \text{and} \quad y = f(x_2)$$

where:

y = attendance at a basketball game

x_1 = population of the area

x_2 = number of games won by the competing team over the past 3 years

If model (a) $[y = f(x_1)]$ yields an (R^2) of (0.61) and model (b) $[y = f(x_2)]$ yields an (R^2) of (0.84), then one can say that (x_2) has a higher explanatory power than (x_1) , and (R^2) as a statistic can be used to select and retain the variables which are more useful in the forecasting equation.

The following remarks set the boundaries for the interpretation of (R^2):

i) (R^2) values tend to be high using time series data and low when using cross-section data. While (R^2) around (0.5) would be acceptable with cross-section data, they would be expected to be around (0.9) with time-series data.

ii) (R^2) can be used for comparing the relative performance of two models only when the dependent variables are the same.

iii) Since (R^2) will increase as more independent variables are added on, whether they are appropriate or not, it is useless in cases where the number of independent variables is not the same.

iv) As more independent variables are added, (R) and (R^2) will always increase. Thus a correction has to be introduced so that the coefficient of determination reflects only the variables which are statistically significant. This can be achieved by using the corrected coefficient of determination:

$$\bar{R}^2 = \text{"R bar - squared"}$$
$$= 1 - \frac{n-1}{n-k}(1 - R^2)$$

v) $(\bar{R}^2)$ can decrease when a new variable is added; it can also become negative. Thus it cannot be interpreted as the proportion of variance explained. However it offers the advantage of accounting for only the variables which are statistically significant. For forecasting purposes, an equation with a higher $(\bar{R}^2)$ will have smaller variance in the error of prediction. In some cases, the model with the highest $(\bar{R}^2)$ may not be the most desirable and discarding a conceptually relevant variable may increase $(\bar{R}^2)$ but bias the other parameter estimates. In this case interpretation of the results may be less meaningful.

(vi) $(\bar{R}^2)$ will decrease if the t-statistic of the added independent variable is less than one in absolute value. In other words, the addition of a new independent variable will always increase (R^2), but will only increase $(\bar{R}^2)$ if it has a t value greater than one. $(\bar{R}^2)$ can be negative, but (R^2) cannot.

(vii) If a variable is eliminated on the basis of a $(t < 1)$, the equation must be re-estimated before judgement can be passed on the remaining variables.

(viii)   Rejecting an independent variable may increase the value of $(\bar{R}^2)$ but may also bias the other parameter estimates.

(ix)   The following figures shows, in a schematic way the extreme cases for the value of $(\bar{R}^2)$.

FIGURE 7.2

SCHEMATIC REPRESENTATION OF VARIOUS DEGREES

OF CORRELATION

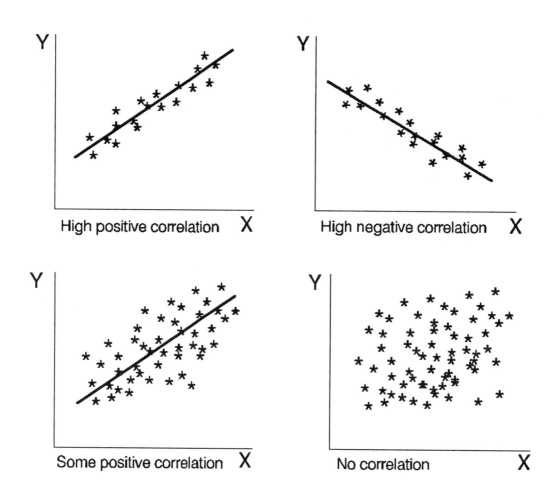

7.3 T-TEST

"How can I know what I think until I represent what I do?"

Anonymous

While *(R) or (R²)* are usually good statistics to evaluate the reliability of the forecasting equation, it is also useful especially when the equation contains more than one independent variable, to evaluate the precision of the regression coefficients. This is done by evaluating the standard errors of the coefficients. The smaller the standard errors, the more reliable the estimates. Usually standard errors are noted below the regression coefficients. The standard error is tested to see if the parameters are significantly different from some hypothesized value of the "true" regression coefficient. This hypothesized value is often taken as zero, and the test is then to determine the probability that a particular estimated regression coefficient could have been obtained by chance when the true value was actually zero. This is done by the use of the "t-statistic" which allows for a test of the statistical significance of each regression coefficient. An Englishman named Gosset developed the theory of the t-distribution. He worked in a brewery, measuring the water content of newly produced stout. He had to sample many barrels of stout to be sure that his sample standard deviation was a stable estimate of the true standard deviation. For some unknown reason he became interested in developing a technique for using smaller samples than before, and his motives led him to develop the "small-sample" statistical theory. Gosset published his paper under the pseudonym "student" and for this reason the t-distribution is often referred to as "Student's t-distribution". The t-statistic may be used to compare the regression coefficient with any number the forecaster has in mind. The most common null hypothesis is that $(b_i=0)$. For this test, the t-ratio is simply the ratio of the regression coefficient to the standard error of the regression coefficient.

$$t = \frac{parameter\ value}{standard\ error}$$

It is generally accepted that the absolute value of t should be greater than, or around two. In this case the parameter is taken to be significantly different from zero and we then fail to reject the hypothesis that the independent variable has no influence on the dependent variable. The t statistics can also be estimated using the coefficient of correlation:

$$t = \frac{r\sqrt{n-2}}{\sqrt{1-r^2}}$$

The following example illustrates the use of the "t-test" in a forecasting exercise. Consider the following model based on the performance of 15 basketball players:

$$y_t = a + b_1 x_1 + b_2 x_2$$

where:

y_t = basketball score during season t

x_1 = average hours of training per season

x_2 = total score in previous two seasons

TABLE 7.1
BASKETBALL PLAYERS PERFORMANCE

Players	y_t	x_1	x_2
1	286	112	590
2	328	147	530
3	293	117	600
4	271	100	590
5	304	133	500
6	289	111	570
7	313	173	510
8	277	103	540
9	286	116	590
10	281	106	520
11	286	99	550
12	269	95	580
13	296	123	610
14	307	125	510
15	302	135	570

The model was estimated by the Least-Squares Method as yielding the following equation (t-values appear under the estimated values):

$$y = 242.00 + 0.639\ x_1 - 0.0464\ x_2$$
$$(5.2) \qquad (5.3) \qquad (-0.68)$$
$$R^2 = 0.768$$

Given the above results, the model will yield bad forecasting values due to the unreliability of the regression coefficient of (X_2) (low t-value). Thus, (X_2) should be rejected and the equation re-estimated. The re-estimated model will have a lower (R^2) but will yield better forecasting results.

7.4 F-TEST

"Largesse! Largesse, O Fortune!
Give or hold at your will
If I've no care for Fortune
Fortune must follow me still!"

R. Kipling

The F-value can be viewed in two ways:

i)   as a test that $(b_1 = b_2 = b_3 = b_K = 0)$. That is, all the regression coefficients are the same and equal to zero, and there is no relationship at all between the dependent variable and the set of independent variables; and

ii)   as a test that $(R^2 = 0)$. There is no reduction in variance resulting from the regression analysis.

The F-value is a ratio defined as:

$$F = \frac{R^2/K-1}{1-R^2/n-K-1}$$

The F-value is meaningless in and of itself. The comparison value is found in the F-tables. An F-test is important because it is a significance test of the entire regression. Using the results of Table 6.1, the value of F is computed as follows:

- (R^2) is the coefficient of determination (0.806),

- (K) is the number of regression coefficients in the model, including the constant term. In this case $(K=2)$, and

- (n) is the number of observations (13).

Thus, we obtain:

$$F = \frac{0.806/(2-1)}{(1-0.806)/(13-2)} = 37.76$$

This value is then compared to critical F-values which can be found in Appendix B. The values obtained from the F-table for 5% and 1% probability are $(F.05=3.74)$ and $(F.01=6.51)$. The hypothesis of "no association between the dependent and the independent variable" is clearly rejected because the calculated $[F(37.76)]$ exceeds the critical values with less than 0.01 probability (6.51), or less than 1% of the time.

7.5 DURBIN-WATSON TEST

"This I ask you, give me the right answer, O Ahura!"

Bartholomac

The D-W statistic is designed to test for serial correlation or autocorrelation in the data. Autocorrelation means that the assumption of independence has been violated and that one observation tends to be correlated with the next. Time series are frequently autocorrelated. This situation is illustrated by the following figure:

FIGURE 7.3

AUTOCORRELATION OF THE RESIDUALS

TIME SERIES

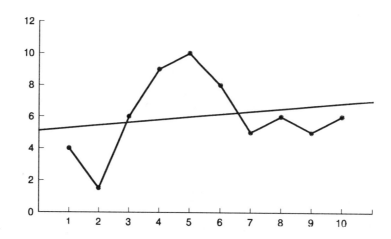

For time periods 3-6 the $(\hat{Y}-Y)$ are all positive, while for the periods 7-10, $[(\hat{Y}-Y)< 0]$ holds. This is called "autocorrelation of the residuals". The D-W statistic provides an indication as to the existence of correlation between the residuals or error terms. It can range between 0 and 4, and has an expected value of 2 if the residuals are independently distributed. As a rule of thumb, if the D-W is around 2 we would tend to reject the existence of correlation in the residuals. The D-W should not be used if there is a lagged dependent variable among the explanatory variables because this will bias the D-W toward 2. The interest of the D-W lies in the fact that usually the existence of correlation in the residuals is indicative of a misspecification in the model. This is a problem for forecasters as they frequently work with time series data, and time series are frequently autocorrelated. The Durbin-Watson statistic is computed by:

$$D\text{-}W = \frac{\sum\limits_{t=2}^{T} (\hat{e}_t - \hat{e}_{t-1})^2}{\sum\limits_{t=1}^{T} \hat{e}_t^2}$$

The numerator cannot include a difference for the first observation in the sample, since no earlier observation is available. When successive values of ($\hat{e}_i$) are close to each other, the D-W will be low, indicating the presence of positive serial correlation. The D-W statistic will lie in the 0-4 range with a value near 2 in cases of no serial correlation. Two limits are given, (d_l) allows one to reject the null hypothesis of no serial correlation whereas, if D-W is greater than (d_u), the null hypothesis is retained. The range between (d_l) and (d_u) leaves us with inconclusive results. Applying the D-W formula to attendance data at a ski resort Table 6.7 we obtain:

TABLE 7.2
CALCULATION OF THE DURBIN-WATSON TEST

Actual Attendance	Estimated			
12	10.53	-1.47	--	2.16
14	16.36	2.36	14.63	5.55
16	16.67	0.67	2.84	0.44
13	10.51	-2.48	9.95	6.17
10	9.92	-0.08	5.77	0.01
18	19.30	1.30	1.92	1.70
21	23.68	2.68	1.89	7.18
24	25.14	1.14	2.38	1.29
22	25.72	3.72	6.66	13.80
30	28.06	-1.94	32.02	3.78
28	25.13	-2.86	0.84	8.19
34	30.98	-3.02	0.03	9.12

Therefore,

$$\sum_{t-2}^{T} (\hat{e}_t - \hat{e}_{t-1})^2 = 78.93, \quad and \quad \sum_{t-1}^{T} e^2_t = 59.39$$

As a result, D-W. = 1.33.

If a lagged value of the dependent variable is used as an independent variable, the D-W statistic is no longer valid. This may not invalidate the use of the regression formula in forecasting, but it does leave tests of significance using t ratios and F statistics with an uncertain meaning. The existence of serial correlation may be due to a "model misspecification" (e.g. using a linear instead of a logarithmic model), to the absence of a key independent variable or to the smoothing of the data. This situation will seriously underestimate the true variance, and the forecasters who use regression when serial correlation is present are misleading themselves as to the significance and accuracy of his forecast. If forecasting the level of a variable poses difficulties and gives rise to "autocorrelation", it is possible to forecast changes in the variable. Series which contain autocorrelation in the residuals when the raw data are used often show no autocorrelation of residuals when first differences are used. Then:

$$Y_t - Y_{t-1} = a + \sum_i b_i (x_{i_t} - x_{i_{t-1}})$$

7.6 STUDY QUESTIONS

1) What is the difference between the correlation coefficient and the coefficient of determination?

2) Provide three examples of "spurious correlation".

3) What is needed to convert a "Statistical Model" to a "Causal Model"?

4)   In a regression model, if you have 16 observations and 3 variables, what will be the degrees of freedom?

5)   Why is it generally recognized that a "t-value" of 2 indicates a statistically acceptable level for the tested variable?

6)   Calculate the F-value when ($R^2 = 0.60$) and (n = 18). Is the F-value meaningful?

7)   What is the use of the Durbin-Watson test? Explain.

7.7 BIBLIOGRAPHY

BROWN, T.L. and B.T. WILKINS
1975   Methods of Improving Recreation Projections, *Journal of Leisure Research*, 7 (3), 225-34.

BURTON, T.L.
1981   You Can't Get There from Here: A Perspective on Recreation Forecasting in Canada, *Recreation Research Review*, 9, 38-43.

CLINE, R.S.
1975   Measuring Travel Volumes and Itineries and Forecasting Future Travel Growth to Individual Pacific Destination. In Ladany, S.P., *Management Science Applications to Leisure Time Operations*, Amsterdam: North-Holland Pub. Co., 134-135.

GRATTON, C. and P. TAYLOR
1992   *Economics and Leisure Services Management*, London: Longman Group UK Ltd.

HENDRY, D.F. and G.E. MIZON
1978   "Serial Correlation as a Convenient Simplification not a Nuisance: A Comment on a Study of the Demand for Money by the Bank of England", *Economic Journal*, 88, 549-63.

HOWORTH, J.T. and S.R. PARKER (eds.)
1976   *Forecasting Leisure Futures*, London: Leisure Studies Assoc.

LAWRENCE, M.J., R.H. EDMUNDSON and M.J. O'CONNOR
1985   "An Examination of the Accuracy of Judgmental Extrapolation of Time Series", *International Journal of Forecasting*, Vol. 1 (1), 25-35.

McCUEN, R.H.
1974   "Spurious Correlation in Estimating Recreation Demand Functions", *Journal of Leisure Research*, Vol. 6, 232-240.

McMASTER, D.J. and M.K. O'LEARY and W.D. COPLIN
1979   "Testing Two Methods of Short-Term Forecasting of Political Violence", *Technological Forecasting and Social Change*, Vol. 14 (2), 115-133.

MAKRIDAKIS, S.G.
1978   *Forecasting: Methods and Applications*, Santa Barbara, CA: Wiley.

MAKRIDAKIS, S.G. and R.L. WINKLER
1983   "Averages of Forecasts: Some Empirical Results", *Management Science*, Vol. 29 (9), 987-996.

MAYER, L.S. and J.A. ROBINSON
1978   "Measures of Association for Multiple Regression Models with Ordinal Predictor Variables", *Sociological Methodology*, Vol. 9, 141-163.

MENDRAS, H.
1981   "Diagnosis and Forecasting in Sociology: Was the Leftist Victory Predictable?", *Futuribles*, Vol. 50, 70-82.

SHERRILL, C.
1983   The Future is Ours to Shape, *Physical Educator*, 40 (1), 44-50.

WERCZBERGER, E.
1984   "Planning in an Uncertain Environment: Stochastic Goal Programming Using the Versatility Criterion", *Socio Economic Planning Sciences*, Vol. 18 (6), 391-398.

WRIGHT, D.
1983   *Missing Data in Time Series: Forecasting Without Interpolation*, Ottawa Ontario: University of Ottawa: Faculty of Administration.

8

FORM AND CONTENT OF THE MODEL

"O body swayed to music, O brightening glance, How can we know the dancer from the dance?"

Yeats

8.1 FORM OF THE MODEL

"Perhaps, after all, the super-observer of the blind men trying to describe the elephant was himself rather blind. Does the skin of the elephant really represent the dividing line between the elephant and its environment? Maybe an understanding of the habitat of the elephant is essential, and perhaps the habitat should be regarded as part of the elephantine system".

C. West Churchman

It is not possible to make a prediction and be sure of obtaining the right answer, because there is no single best theory or model to explain a phenomenon. Thus, there is no unique prediction and each model will yield a different forecast. Moreover, there is no set rule to follow in selecting the form of the model. This is an empirical issue and cannot be resolved by a priori guidelines. There is a temptation to experiment blindly with a large variety of functional forms and retain the form which will yield a "good fit". Such an approach discovers hypotheses rather than tests them. The model then generates parameter estimates tailored to the observed data rather than to the underlying universe. Of course one should avoid fits which are statistically correct but not necessarily in harmony with the existing theory.

Numerous forms may be applied. However, the following forms are most popular and reflect quite well the behaviour of many sports and recreation activities.

1)   **Linear**

The linear form is simple and easy to understand but assumes, of course, a constant relationship while sometimes the "real" situation does not follow a linear trend. The basic linear equation is :

$$y_t = a + bx_t$$

Often the forecaster would select a linear form based on visual inspection of a scatter diagram. However, a technique using first-order differences can be used to ascertain whether a linear equation, a second-degree polynomial, or a higher-degree equation should be selected. First-order differences are defined as:

$$\Delta Y_t = Y_t - Y_{t-1}$$

- If the difference between observations is relatively constant, a linear trend is appropriate, for example consider the following time series:

$$2,4,6,8,10,12,14$$

The first differences are *2, 2, 2, 2, 2, 2*. This new series is stationary, clearly indicating a perfect linear trend.

- In some cases a second-degree polynomial fits the trend better. This can be verified if the second difference of a series is stationary. The second difference is defined as:

$$\Delta^2 Y_t = \Delta Y_t - \Delta Y_{t-1}$$

The following example illustrates this situation:

TABLE 8.1

FIRST AND SECOND DIFFERENCES

Y_t	First Differences	Second Differences
15	--	--
28	13	4
45	17	4
66	21	4
91	25	4
120	29	4
153	33	4
190	37	4
231	41	4
276	45	4
325	49	4
378	53	4

One may fit a linear time trend to the original Y_t series. This results in the following regression:

$$Y_t = 54.667 + 33.00 \text{ time}$$
$$(-3.84) \quad (17.08)$$
$$R^2 = 0.967 \quad \text{D-W.} = 0.33$$

The time trend is significant and the R-square values are very high. However, the unusually low value of the Durbin-Watson statistic suggest a specification problem. Thus, if we use first differences and plot the data, the series would be equally spaced, i.e. increases by 4 units per time interval. Running a regression in such a case would produce a perfect $R^2(1)$ and the estimation of (y) would simply be equal to a constant (4) plus 2

y_{t-1} and minus y_{t-2}. Using Table 8.1, the forecast of $y_t = 66$ would amount to : $66 = 4 + 2 (45)-28$.

In some cases an "inverse linear" relationship can be used:

$$y_t = a + \frac{b}{x}$$

This form can be converted into an inverse linear:

$$y_t = a + b \left(\frac{1}{x}\right)$$

Data creating allows nonlinearities to be introduced into a linear model. Assume that there is an multiplicative interaction between two independent variables:

$$(x_{1j})(x_{2j}) = x_j^2$$

The basic relationship between (y) and (x_j) becomes quadratic:

$$y = a + b_1 x_j + b_2 x_j^2$$

However, it is still a linear regression since it can be arbitrarily defined as:

$$z_j = x_j^2$$

and can be estimated by a linear form:

$$y = a + b_1 x_j + b_2 z_j + \varepsilon$$

The linear form is widely used for the following reasons:

- from a pragmatic point of view, unless one has reasons to judge otherwise, the linear model represents a reasonable assumption;

- the linear model is a useful first step in hypothesis testing;

- it is simple to comprehend;

- many relationships are fundamentally governed by linear process; and

- the linear regression model only requires that there be linearity with respect to the parameters to be estimated. If the model is non-linear, it may be possible to transform the variables.

2)   **Straight-Line Geometric Trend**

Straight lines are sometimes not adequate, especially in a situation when a market share increases significantly during the growth process, and competitive or institutional forces are expected to exert increased influence, slowing down or even stopping further growth.

In such cases "saturation" is experienced and the growth rate decreases, changing the straight line into a flattening curve on the semi-logarithmic. One way of correcting for a changing growth rate is to plot the time series of the growth rate on semi-logarithmic paper and extrapolate it to estimate future rates. A growth rate following a downward straight line trend would produce a smoothly saturating growth curve. So, when the scatter diagram plotted on a semilogarithmic grid approximates a straight line, this is indicative of a constant rate of change year by year, as contrasted to an arithmetic change year by year for a straight-line trend. The following formula describes this situation:

$$log\ Y = a + bx$$

3)   **Parabola**

A parabola is a function which may be fitted to many non-linear relationships. The general form of the parabola is:

$$y = a + b_1x_1 + b_2x_1^2$$

For convenience (x_1^2) may be defined as (x_2) and can then be solved in the same way as a three-variable regression model. The regression is then run as:

$$y = a + b_1x_1 + b_2x_2$$

Using data from Table 6.1 we obtain the following results:

$$Log\ Quantity = 38.62 - 2.165\ log\ (Price)^2$$
$$(72.4)\ \ (-52.4)$$
$$R^2 = 0.996 \qquad\qquad D\text{-}W. = 1.70$$

Plotting the data indicates a negative relationship with the charge to the users: the higher the charge, the lower the quantity demanded.

The shape of the scatter diagram between y an x will depend on the signs of a, b_1 and b_2. Let's assume 'a' is positive in all cases below. If both b_i are positive, then a positive relationship, increasing at an increasing rate, will be detected. If b_2 and b_1 are both negative, the scatter diagram will show a negative relationship between y and x_1. If b_1 > 0, and b_2 < 0, then the scatter diagram may yield ambiguous results in a limited sample size.

4)   **Hyperbola**

This curve is frequently encountered in data relating cost to attendance or participation. The equation of this curve often appears in the form:

$$y = a + \frac{b}{x}$$

Graphically, this is illustrated in Figure 8.1:

FIGURE 8.1
RELATIONSHIP BETWEEN COSTS AND PARTICIPATION
HYPERBOLA

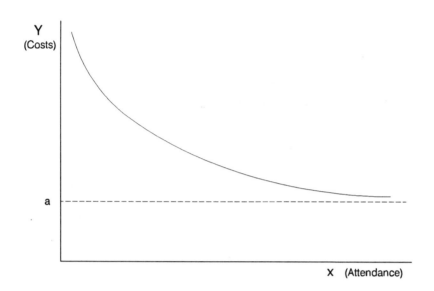

$$0 < b < 1 \; ; \; a > 0$$

The main characteristic of this curve is that it approaches but never reaches limiting values in both the (x) and the (y) dimensions. This case is typically exemplified by the relationship between attendance and the costs incurred:

y = unit cost per swimmer

a = fixed cost

b = variable cost

x = attendance

Thus unit cost is equal to a variable cost (a), plus a proportion of the fixed costs in relation to attendance. Estimating this relationship requires a transformation to a linear form, where:

$$Z = \frac{1}{x}$$

To illustrate the hyperbolic model consider the following relationships between "participation" and "fees", as indicated in Table 8.2:

TABLE 8.2

PARTICIPATION AND FEES

Season	Participation	Fees
1	269	1.50
2	239	2.00
3	206	2.50
4	218	2.75
5	215	2.85
6	237	2.85
7	158	3.40
8	185	4.00
9	151	4.25
10	165	4.50
11	156	4.90
12	152	5.40
13	175	5.50
14	157	5.70
15	169	6.30

If we apply a linear form, we obtain:

$$\text{Participation} = 273.461 - 21.403 \text{ Fees}$$
$$(16.7) \quad (-5.4)$$
$$R^2 = 0.694 \quad D\text{-}W = 1.70$$

The coefficient of the "fees" variable is negative as expected and the R^2 is acceptable. However, an improvement can be made if a hyperbolic form is used. The hyperbolic specification will take the form:

$$\text{Participation} = a + \frac{b}{\text{Fees}}$$

This time, b is expected to be positive, since the hyperbolic form takes care of the negative relationship. The estimation of this equation yields:

$$\text{Participation} = 117.045 + 242.537 / \text{Fees}$$
$$(10.83) \quad (7.41)$$
$$R^2 = 0.809 \quad \text{D-W.} = 2.38$$

The R-square values improved, and the coefficient in front of the fee variable carries a positive and significant sign. In this case, the hyperbolic model should be prefered to the previous linear form.

5)   **Logarithmic**

In some situations, data plotted on an ordinary scatter diagram would exhibit curvilinear patterns and the possibility of multiplicative rather than additive relationships. When this occurs, as it frequently does, simple methods exist for transforming a multiplicative relationship into an additive one by using either logarithms, reciprocals, roots or powers, or logarithms of logarithms. For example, consider the following multiplicative relationship which is the well-known compound interest function:

$$y = ab^x$$

In the above model, (b) is a positive constant raised to the power (*x*) which measures the number of time periods beyond the base year and (a) is a constant multiple. If (*x*) was negative (y = ab⁻ˣ) this would indicate that (y) is decreasing over time.

On ordinary graph paper this equation plots as a curved line. However, if the equation is plotted on logarithmic paper, or if the logarithm of the variables are scaled on arithmetic paper, the following additive relationship is obtained:

$$\log y = \log a + x \log b$$

In this form, the analysis could be run by the graphic method and straight lines used, since the equation is linear in logarithms. It can simply be stated that:

$$y = \log y, \quad a = \log a, \quad and \quad b = \log b.$$

We then have the linear form:

$$y = a + bx$$

6) **Log-linear**

In some situations the relationship is not linear, not only in one variable but in two. This is often the case with price (*x*) and quantity demanded (*y*), and the function may be as follows:

$$y = a\,x^b$$

By taking the logs of this function we obtain:

$$\log y = \log a + b \log x$$

Using data from Table 6.1 (demand relationship), we estimate the following:

$$\log \text{ quantity} = 38.621 - 4.332 \log \text{ price}$$
$$(72.4) \qquad (-52.4)$$
$$R^2 = 0.996 \qquad \text{D-W.} = 1.70$$

Thus a decrease in price of 1% would increase the quantity demanded by 4.33%.

The log form of this statistical relationship is linear and may fit in the usual way. When logarithmic data are used, because both the logs and the associated errors get very large quickly as one moves upward on the scale, the forecaster has to be careful not to go far beyond the domain of the data points.

7)   **Modified Exponential Curve**

This curve is somewhat similar to the compound growth curve and its formula is:

$$y = k + aX^b$$

The formula implies that (*X*) is raised to the power (b) rather than the other way around.

It is similar to the exponential growth pattern and gives the forecaster another possible curve to check for it. This situation is illustrated in Figures 8.2 and 8.3:

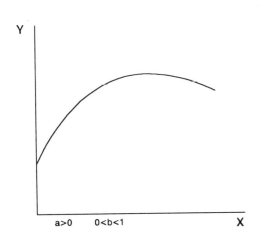

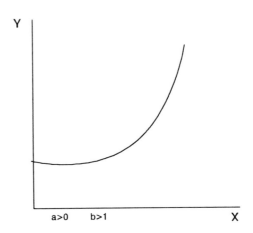

To estimate (a) and (b) through regression analysis, the curve can be transformed to a linear form:

$$\log(y - K) = \log(a) + b\log(X)$$

8)   **Logistic Curve**

This curve, often referred to as the S-shaped curve, is applicable to situations characterised by a starting low growth rate, followed by accelerating growth, and then decelerating growth as the limit is approached. The formula for this curve is:

$$y = \frac{1}{(\frac{1}{K} + ab^x)}$$

Its linear conversion is:

$$\log(\frac{1}{y} - \frac{1}{K}) = \log(a) + \log(b)x$$

8.2 DATA

"No data yet" he answered. "It is a capital mistake to theorize before you have all the evidence. It biases the judgement".

Sherlock Holmes in Sir A.C. Doyle's, A Study in Scarlet

Data by definition are quantitative expressions of the measurement of some object under study. The process of estimating a regression equation requires data on all the variables in the model. Data can be expressed in different forms:

1) **Qualitative Nature**

While qualitative information is often needed to reflect specific characteristics of a situation, for forecasting purposes a numerical transformation is required. For instance:

-   "users' satisfaction" can be measured on a scale of 0 to 10, where 0 denotes "full satisfaction" and 10 denotes "total non-satisfaction";
-   "accessibility" can be expressed as a weighted distance between a recreation site and population centres; and
-   "attitudes" can be measured on a Likert scale.

2)   **Proxy Variables**

In some cases, the specified variable cannot be measured or may simply be too costly to measure. In these cases, the variable would be substituted by another variable - a proxy. Examples of proxy variables follow:

- the use of the number of employees as a proxy for "size";
- miles of trails as a proxy for "capacity";
- years of service as a proxy for "experience";
- years of schooling as a proxy for "income"; and/or
- time trend as a proxy for "socio-economic" changes.

3)   **Dummy Variables**

In some situations the forecaster cannot quantify the information, as in the case of:

man	vs	woman
resident	vs	non-resident
participant	vs	non-participant
private	vs	public

In such cases, when the answer is "either/or", a proxy variable is introduced which is referred to as a "dummy" variable. This variable modifies the information into discrete categories by assuming dummy values (0 or 1) for each of the categories. If there are (n) categories to distinguish, it would take at most (n -1) dummy variables. The (n^{th}) category would then be the excluded one, and the coefficients of the dummies included would be measuring the partial influence of those categories relative to the excluded one.

In some situations, dummy variables are used to take into account a shift in the distribution of the observations. This is illustrated by Figure 8.4:

FIGURE 8.4

EXAMPLE OF CASE WHERE A DUMMY VARIABLE IS REQUIRED

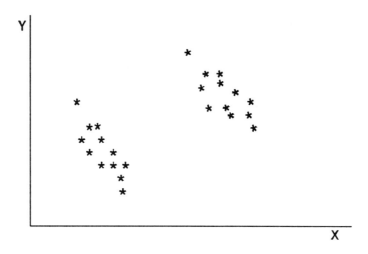

A visual inspection of the data reveals two clusters of points which seem to have a roughly similar slope. An equation containing a dummy variable will then be applied, and the model would take the form:

$$y = a + b_1 x + b_2 D$$

For each of the *(x),(y)* pairs in the upper cluster, (D) would be assigned a value of one. Similarly, for each of the *(x),(y)* pairs in the lower cluster, (D) would have the value of zero. The assignment of zero-one is arbitrary and could easily be reversed. This technique would in effect allow estimation of the *(x),(y)* relationship from all of the data available and at the same time take out the influence of the shift in the relationship which obviously exists.

8.3 DATA TRANSFORMATION

"This statistical jungle can sometimes be more difficult to penetrate than a statistical desert".

D.A. Glenn

Forecasting implies trend extrapolation at a constant rate. This constant rate may refer to:

- the numerical rate of increase;
- the percentage rate of increase;
- the doubling rate; or
- any other rate of change which is treated as constant and reflects the analyzed trend, such as first differences or logarithms.

Thus, the trend often hides a systematic movement in the data series requiring some data transformation to make the trends apparent. A few of these transformations are presented below:

1) **Deviations from the Mean**

By definition, a trend is a "general tendency" which is centred around an average. Thus all the variations around the mean are less important than the "core" of the series. For example, participation at an outdoor sports event is expected to vary with climate conditions. However, it has been observed that deviations from the mean have a greater impact on participation than the mean itself. In other words, if the month of June has an average temperature of, say 70 F, deviations from this average have a greater impact on participation than the absolute level. The same reasoning is applicable to rainfall.

The mean is defined as:

$$\bar{x} = \frac{\sum\limits_{i=1}^{n} x_i}{N}$$

the deviation from the mean (x_i) is defined as:

$$x_i = x_i - \bar{x}$$

2)   **Percentage Rate of Change**

The percentage rate of change is defined as:

$$\frac{(t_i - t_0)}{t_0} \; X \;\; 100$$

where:

t_i = present year

t_0 = previous year

This method is useful when the series has a marked growth, as is the case in situations where the growth is mainly exponential. In this case, the percentage change transforms an exponentially growing series into one that is constant. The constant series is often much easier to analyze. The percentage changes in the data from the preceding year are also known as "link relatives". Percentage change is particularly useful when the amount in which the variable increases over time depends on the size of the variable.

3)   **First Difference**

Many variables increase over time. In such cases, using the absolute level will simply indicate that the variable is indeed growing. Variations of the variable, other than the growth, will be hidden by the growth. In these situations a data transformation would bring out the variability in the variable. This can be achieved by calculating the "first difference" of the data, which is defined as:

$$\Delta x_t = x_t - x_{t-1}$$

The first difference is a needed data transformation when using time series data which have a strong trend. In this case, if first differences are not used, the forecaster will only capture the long trend. Short term changes will not be captured. Moreover, many time series data which contain autocorrelation in the residuals when the raw data are used, exhibit no autocorrelation of residuals from a regression using first differences. Forecasting changes in the variable can be achieved with a greater degree of confidence.

In the area of sports and recreation, many variables show a steady increase over time. Examples of this situation comprise participation in all types of recreational activities (e.g. jogging, sailing, skiing, etc.). Thus participation will show a continuous growth over time. However, this growth might not necessarily have the same magnitude, and it is therefore essential to transform the variable in order to bring out the variations. Often first differences are used when the absolute level of the series is quite high and variations based on these levels are modest. For instance, if total participation in all sports activities shows a long term growth but in the short term some variations in the growth are evident, then projecting the absolute level would yield poor results for short term changes. The forecast will capture the long term trend but will fail to predict accurately year-to-year changes. In such a case, the use of first differences would improve the results.   When the first differences are used, the mathematically derived function can be employed to forecast the "change" rather than the absolute level.

4) Ratios

This is a useful transformation, because a variable often will change over time, but will not change relative to another variable. Examples of the most popular ratios are:

- unemployment rates;
- crime rates;
- participation rates; and
- market penetration rates.

5) Logarithm

When a series grows exponentially, its logarithm grows linearly and is more easily analyzed. Moreover, using logarithms will make the series more smoother and trends will be seen more easily. The mean is the center of the series and determines the level of the series. Movement around the mean is more important than the actual level itself. Taking logarithms is also used to stabilize the variance of the series in levels. Furthermore, the first difference of a logarithmic series is approximately equal to the percentage growth rate. Therefore, taking the logarithm makes more sense when percentage changes in a variable is more important than the absolute changes.

6) Lagged Variables

Participation in recreation and sports activities often exhibit a time lag. For example, the participation function might be specified as follows:

$$P_t = a + b Y_{t-1}$$

where present participation (P_t) is related to income earned last year (Y_{t-1}). Time lags are not uncommon. Individuals do not always change their participation habits as soon as a specific explanatory variable is altered. There may be socio-economic reasons, or simply their behaviour is affected by previous psychological factors. A lagged model offers obvious advantages for the forecaster. When data for the independent variable for the present period are used, the calculation obviously yields an estimate of the forecast variable in period (t + 1), the period to be forecast. The danger with lagged variables is when the same variable appears on both sides. No competent forecaster would regress a variable on itself. But it is almost sound to suggest that "previous" participation determines "present" participation. This introduces obvious serial correlation, and the results would be at best misleading. For forecasting purposes, limited use should be made of lagged variables.

7)   **Seasonal Variations**

In some situations, the data indicate the existence of seasonal variations. This can be detected simply by plotting the new data. Such phenomena are exemplified in:

- Tourist arrivals;
- Visits to national parks;
- Outdoor swimming; and
- Sport games.

If the variable being used in the forecast changes substantially from month to month and the months tend to be similar in successive years, then the model may take the following form:

$$\hat{Y}_{t+1} = Y_{t-11}$$

This model states that for the next month the variable will take on the same value it did in the corresponding month, one year ago.

8.4 SELECTION OF THE INDEPENDENT VARIABLES

"That's enough to begin with, Humpty Dumpty interrupted: there are plenty of hard words there".

Lewis Carroll, *Through the Looking-Glass*

The forecaster is often faced with a situation where several independent variables may be introduced into the forecasting model. The forecaster is interested in selecting three or four variables which will yield the best results. This can be achieved by the following techniques:

1) **Filtering**

The most accurate method for selecting the explanatory variables is to test all possible regression equations and to choose the best. However, this is extremely time consuming. Indeed, if (p) explanatory variables are considered, the total number of equations is generally equal to:

$$2^p - 1$$

If we have 10 explanatory variables, we obtain 1,023 equations and 1,048,575 equations for 20 explanatory variables.

2) Backward Elimination

All explanatory variables are considered in one single equation, and the significance of each variable is tested by the t statistic. Only the variables which have the higher level of statistical significance are retained. Thus:

$$y = f(x_1, x_2, x_3, \ldots, x_n)$$

This relationship will be estimated by the following regression equation:

$$y = a + b_1x_1 + b_2x_2 + b_3x_3, \ldots + b_nx_n$$

The variables will be selected if:

$$t_i = \frac{bi}{\sigma_{bi}} > 2$$

If (t_i) is (< 2), (x_i) will be rejected.

This method is cumbersome when the explanatory variables exceed seven or eight variables. Data on expenditures at Ouhala Camp (CAMP), average number of campers per weekend (NUMBER), and the number of traffic accidents (ACC) on the highway leading to the camp ground will be used to explain the method.

TABLE 8.3

OUHALA CAMP REVENUES

Season	Camp ($'000)	Number (#)	ACC (#)
1	49.32	150	26
2	44.54	110	43
3	35.50	90	12
4	36.02	60	7
5	39.72	80	5
6	49.63	120	23
7	41.56	100	27
8	75.92	250	11
9	49.22	140	17
10	56.46	180	12
11	84.12	290	3
12	63.76	240	21
13	82.48	300	25
14	45.98	140	34
15	49.85	160	18

As the first step include both NUMBER and ACC in the regression.

$$CAMP = 22.687 + 0.203 \text{ NUMBER} - 0.092 \text{ ACC}$$

$$(8.34) \quad (17.13) \quad (-1.13)$$

$$R^2 = 0.961 \quad \text{D-W.} = 2.39$$

Both independent variables have the expected sign. However, the t- value on the ACC variable is not greater than 2. Therefore, this variable may be dropped from the regression and a bivariate regression may be run.

$$\text{CAMP} = 20.718 + 0.205 \text{ NUMBER}$$
$$(9.84) \quad (17.17)$$
$$R^2 = 0.958 \qquad \text{D-W.} = 2.10$$

The exclusion of ACC did not cause a change in the coefficient of NUMBER and its significance. Even though R^2 dropped very slightly, the bivariate regression gives a very good fit.

3)   **Forward Selection**

Explanatory variables will be introduced until the regression equation deteriorates. The explanatory variable which has the highest correlation is selected, and then the next one, and we observe the change in t-statistic. The following steps are required:

.   First step: $y = a + b_1 x_1$

the variables are ranked on the basis of the correlation coefficient. If (R_i) is the correlation coefficient between (y) and (x_i) then we have $(R_2 > R_1 > R_4 > ... > ...)$

Then if:

$$t_1 = \frac{b_1}{\sigma_{b_1}} > 2$$

we retain (x_1), otherwise (x_1) is rejected.

Second step: $y = a + b_1x_1 + b_2x_2$

if (t_1) or $(t_2 <)$ we reject (x_1) and (x_2) and so on ...

Using the previous data from 'Ouhala Camp', the simple correlation coefficients are calculated as follows:

TABLE 8.4
CORRELATION MATRIX (R)
OUHALA CAMP

	Camp	Number	ACC
Camp	--		
Number	0.9788	--	
ACC	-0.1703	-0.1095	--

This method is similar to the backward elimination. First, include the variable with the highest simple correlation with the dependent variable. In this case, it is NUMBER, with R = 0.9788. Then, run the bivariate regression.

$$CAMP = 20.718 + 0.205 \text{ NUMBER}$$
$$(9.84) \quad (17.17)$$
$$R^2 = 0.958 \quad D\text{-}W. = 2.10$$

Then, introduce the next variable and run the three variable regression, and so on.

$$CAMP = 22.687 + 0.203 \text{ NUMBER} - 0.092 \text{ ACC}$$
$$(8.34) \quad (17.13) \quad (-1.13)$$
$$R^2 = 0.961 \quad D\text{-}W. = 2.39$$

This output is identical to the backward elimination method, but in reverse order.

4) **Stepwise Regression**

This method is highly similar to the "Forward Selection" with the possibility of eliminating a variable retained previously, if its level of significance decreases. In our case, the forward selection and stepwise regression produce the same results. This is because, NUMBER is very strongly correlated with CAMP, and the correlation between NUMBER and ACC is low and insignificant ($R = -0.1095$). In general, when there are more than two independent variables or when the independent variables are correlated among themselves, the stepwise regression may cause the elimination of a variable retained previously. That is, if a previously significant variable becomes insignificant, or changes its sign upon the introduction of another variable, then this variable may be excluded. As a result, only those variables which are robust in their signs and significance levels will be included in the final specification. However, one must be careful about the multicollinearity problem.

5) **Stagewise Regression**

Initially, the variable with the highest correlation coefficient is retained. Then the regression equation is estimated and the residuals are considered as variables. The equation best correlated with the first residual is selected. A new equation with two variables will produce new residuals, and so on. More specifically:

- Estimate (R_i) [simple correlation coefficients between (y) and the different (x_i)];
- Select (x_j) based on $[R_j = Max \{R_i \}]$;
- Residual analysis using the regression of (y) on (x_j);

· Estimate (R_i) : the simple correlation coefficient between (ε_1) and the different (x_i)

$$y = a + b_j x_j + \varepsilon_1$$

· Select (x_h) so that $[R'_h = Max \ \{R'_i\}]$; and
· Estimate the residuals of the regression equation of (y) and $(x_j, (x_h)$ and so on.

$$y = a + b_1 x_j + b_2 x_h + \varepsilon_2$$

The analysis of the residuals at each stage enables us to obtain maximum information from the explanatory variables while minimizing the inter-correlations. The selection of the independent variables should also take into consideration the "reasonableness" of the choice, which should be guided by the following:

i) *Ability to forecast the independent variable.* Only those independent variables which can be forecasted within a reasonable degree of accuracy should be used in the forecast. As forecasts of independent variables generally come from other sources, it is often easy to forget that the estimating procedure is only as good as the quality of the future estimates of the independent variables.

ii) *Stability.* The assumption of stability over time is generally made when forecasting with regression equations. It is extremely important that independent variables which contribute to the stability of the relationships over time be chosen.

iii)   *Logic of Variables.* Only those variables which are reasonably related to the dependent variable should be permitted to enter the forecasting equation. It is important that completely illogical independent variables be removed before the forecasting process begins. Some independent variables enter into an equation due to association within the data alone. Such association between independent and dependent variables may be caused merely by chance. In order to have a meaningful relationship and some reasonable degree of confidence in the forecast, the relationship should be causative.

iv)   *Signs of the independent variables.* Logic must be considered when examining the positive or negative contribution of the independent variables in a regression equation. In many instances, the contribution to the estimate of the dependent variable is illogical. For example, in equations developed to forecast participation in recreational and sport activities, income should be positively correlated to participation. But the relationship is seldom linear, and it might be logical to introduce the square value of income to take into consideration the negative effect of income on participation when it exceeds a certain level.

To illustrate stagewise regression, let us introduce another independent variable, AREA, which indicates the average number of campers per weekend in the surrounding area excluding campers from Ouhala Camp. Assume that this variable is correlated with NUMBER, and is able to explain CAMP, in the absence of NUMBER.

TABLE 8.5

OTHER CAMPERS IN THE AREA

Season	Area
1	370
2	140
3	100
4	110
5	60
6	90
7	180
8	210
9	170
10	130
11	280
12	140
13	220
14	200
15	80

The new simple correlation matrix is as follows:

TABLE 8.6
CORRELATION MATRIX (R)
OUHALA CAMP AND AREA

	Camp	Number	Area	ACC
Camp	--			
Number	0.9787	--		
Area	0.4803	0.4877	--	
ACC	-0.1703	0.1095	0.1684	--

NUMBER has the highest correlation with CAMP. Therefore, the bivariate regression should be calculated, and the residuals estimated. The following Table 8.7 shows the actual, fitted, and the residuals from this regression.

TABLE 8.7

RESULTS OF THE BIVARIATE REGRESSION

OUHALA CAMP REVENUES

Actual	Estimates	Residual
49.32	51.42	-2.10
44.54	43.23	1.31
35.50	39.14	-3.64
36.02	33.00	3.02
39.72	37.09	2.63
49.63	45.28	4.35
41.56	41.19	0.37
75.92	71.89	4.03
49.22	49.38	-0.16
56.46	57.56	-1.10
84.12	80.08	4.04
63.76	69.85	-6.09
82.48	82.13	0.35
45.98	49.38	-3.39
49.85	53.47	-3.62

Now, calculate the simple correlations between the residuals (RESID1), and each of AREA and ACC.

Correlation Coefficients:	ACC	AREA
RESID1:	-0.3075	0.0145

Run the regression: $(CAMP + RESID1) = a + b\ ACC$

$$(CAMP + RESID1) = 59.938 - 0.334\ ACC$$

$$(6.69)\quad (-0.81)$$

$$R^2 = 0.04 \qquad D\text{-}W. = 1.72$$

This regression is not significant. The next stage is to calculate the residuals from this regression, RESID2, and create a new dependent variable, $(CAMP + RESID1 + RESID2)$. Then, a regression involving AREA on this dependent variable is run. The estimated results are:

$$(CAMP + RESID1 + RESID2) = 59.666 + 0.2876\ AREA$$

$$(2.19)\quad (1.94)$$

$$R^2 = 0.225 \qquad D\text{-}W. = 1.86$$

This stage shows that AREA has a positive significant effect. (Insignificant at 5% but significant at 10%. Check the t-tables).

Therefore, one can run the following regression:

$$CAMP = a + b_1\ NUMBER + b_2\ AREA$$

The estimation yields:

$$CAMP = 20.657 + 0.2043\ NUMBER + 0.00076\ AREA$$

$$(14.38)\qquad\qquad (0.06)$$

$$R^2 = 0.958 \qquad D\text{-}W. = 2.10$$

Now, the coefficient of AREA changes substantially, and the variable becomes highly insignificant. Note that the coefficient and the t-value of the NUMBER variable is not affected by the inclusion of AREA in the regression. Therefore, one can conclude that the bivariate model $CAMP = f\ (NUMBER)$ best fits the data.

1) "While reality seldom follows a linear trend, it can often be reasonably approximated by a linear function". Comment on this statement.

2) In which situations is a linear form totally inacceptable for forecasting purposes? Provide a numerical example with 15 observations. Use a scatter diagram to illustrate your case.

3) Shown below are total recreation expenditures of the municipality of Bonneville:

TABLE 8.8
BONNEVILLE RECREATION EXPENDITURES

Year	Expenditures (Thousands $)
1	60
2	68
3	76
4	89
5	103
6	105
7	110
8	114
9	121
10	132

i) What type of curve does this series appear to fit best?

ii)   Estimate the parameters of the curve using the Least-Squares Method.

iii)   Calculate (R) and (R^2).

iv)   Prepare a forecast for each of the 3 years following year 10.

v)   Identify any judgmental factors you used to supplement the statistical analysis.

vi)   Compare the actual figures with the forecasts for the 10 years period.

4)   Provide a numerical example of a situation where a logarithmic function would yield better forecasting results.

5)   What is a "dummy variable"? Provide an example of a dummy variable in a sport activity.

6)   For a basketball player what would be a good proxy for "experience"?

7)   When is it desirable to transform data using the "percentage rate of change"? Provide an example.

8)   What are the limitations of using "lagged variables"?

9)   "Any increase in the number of independent variables will increase the value of the correlation coefficient (R)". Do you agree with this statement? Is it always desirable to obtain a higher correlation coefficient?

10) For forecasting purpose why is it recommended to use the minimum number of independent variables? Is there a trade-off between a higher value of (R) and fewer independent variables?

8.6 BIBLIOGRAPHY

FIRTH, M.A.
1977   *Forecasting Methods in Business and Management*. London: Edward Arnold.

FLORES, B.E. and E.M. WHITE
1989   "Subjective versus Objective combining of Forecasts: An Experiment", *Journal of Forecasting*, Vol. 8 (3), 331-341.

HARVEY, A.C. and P.C. YOUNG, and J. LEDOLTER
1984   "A Unified View of Statistical Forecasting Procedures", *Journal of Forecasting*, Vol. 3 (3), 245-275.

JENKINS, G.M.
1982   "Some Practical Aspects of Forecasting in Organizations", *Journal of Forecasting*, Vol. 1, 3-21.

McGOWAN, I.
1986   "The Use of Growth Curves in Forecasting Market Development", *Journal of Forecasting*, Vol. 5, 69-72.

PETERSON, G.L., D.J. STYNES and J.R. ARNOLD
1985   "The Stability of a Recreation Demand Model Over Time", *Journal of Leisure Research*, Vol. 17, 121-132.

TANAKA, Y.
1983   "Some Criteria for Variable Selection in Factor Analysis", *Behaviormetrika*, Vol. 13, 31-45.

9

QUALITY OF FORECASTS

"And I know that anything more which you may say will be vain. Yet speak, if you have anything to say."

Plato (Crito)

9.1 ATTRIBUTES OF A GOOD FORECAST

"The optimal strategy is just the simple tactic of attempting to do one's best on a purely local basis".

A. Wald

The major aim of forecasting is to aid the decision-making processes and to reduce uncertainty. To achieve this goal, a forecast should possess the following characteristics:

1)   **Accuracy**

While, in general, accuracy is perceived as the main requirement for a forecast, there are variations in its level. For instance, if the break-even point of sale of a sporting goods store is $500,000 per year, then a forecast of $550,000 would yield profits, and a forecast of $450,000 would mean that the company would be incurring significant losses.

2)   **Simplicity**

Simplicity is a desirable characteristic of a forecasting model because:

- complicated methods are often difficult to apply and cumbersome;
- while the real world is complex, a simple method bridges the gap and erases the understanding of the real-life situation; and
- simple methods are easier to assess.

3)   **Explanatory Variables**

The validity of regression analysis depends not only on the strength of the relationship between the dependent variable and each explanatory variable, but also on the accuracy of the projection of these explanatory variables.

The predicted values are highly enhanced if they are related to the dependent variable by a time lag. In this case the future values of the predicted variable depend on already historical values of the basic trends.

4)   **Costs**

Costs involved in selecting a forecasting technique can vary enormously. They include the costs of developing models and systems, the costs of data collection, and the operating costs. For short term decisions, there is seldom time to collect new data. Thus, the forecasting method chosen would be one which could make best use of existing information. In general, management has to weigh the costs involved in acquiring data against the benefits obtained in using this data in the appropriate model.

9.2 PITFALLS

"You must talk to me, Mr. Coolidge, I made a bet today that I could get more than two words out of you".

"You lose" said the Vice-President with a poker face, and let it go at that.

Ishbel Ross <u>Grace Coolidge</u>

While regression analysis is a powerful forecasting tool, it has many pitfalls that can be avoided by combining the technique with judgement and common sense. In fact, there is always an element of risk in any forecast. However, a carefully designed forecasting model, including the attributes which were highlighted in the previous section, could reduce that risk and yield reliable forecasts which are not only statistically sound but also have valid operational foundations. Thus, using regression analysis to forecast has to be complemented by additional knowledge about the environment. Statistical curve fitting is not sufficient to produce an accurate forecast. In forecasting sports and recreation activities, there are several pitfalls which could invalidate the results or reduce the value of the forecasts. These can be grouped under the following:

1) Realism

In order to have confidence in using the model for predictive purposes, it is essential that the relationships of the model are logical and agree with observed behavior patterns. The model should rest on solid theoretical foundations or on observed behavior, and should not merely be the product of a clever statistical manipulation for the following two reasons:

i)   Statistical manipulation can yield good results, but the results might not be stable and the relationship is not necessarily valid when another set of data is used.

ii)   A lack of logical link between the dependent variable and the independent variable or variables is conducive to the rejection of the relationship.

Thus, the regression equation should be in harmony with the real-world facts. To illustrate this rule, assume that a ski resort manager was able to establish a sound relationship between the number of skiers and the publicity budget. Thus, in an attempt to increase demand, he boosts his publicity budget by a factor of five. While, statistically speaking, such an increase should strongly increase the level of demand, the relationship might not hold in the real world due to competition from other ski resorts, supply constraints, or simply the overall size of the market. Thus, while the forecast is correct in terms of linear regression, it is unrealistic in terms of real-world facts. Common sense has to be used, and forecast data should not be too far from the envelope of the empirically derived data. Merely projecting the statistical relationship is unrealistic, and judgement should be exercised to avoid falling into statistical traps.

2)   Setting the Number of Variables

In the choice of independent variables, the logic of the proposed relationship should be considered carefully. It is important to realize that this choice should be based on considerable subjective reasoning, rather than relying on the computer program alone to sift the data and "find" a relationship.

In the case of the "stepwise" analysis, the computer will, at each step, enter into the equation the variable which will provide the greatest reduction in the residual sum of squares. This procedure considers only the associative relationship between the independent and dependent variables and, as such, the relationship may be caused only by chance. Indeed, some independent variables enter into an equation due to association within the data alone. Such association between independent and dependent variables may be merely caused by chance. In order to have a meaningful relationship and some reasonable degree of confidence in the forecast, the relationship should be causative. Selecting the proper number of variables should be given careful consideration. There are dangers involved both in selecting too many and too few variables.

3)   **Selecting Too Many Variables**

With too many variables, the model becomes difficult to handle. "Forecasting" models are different from "explanatory" models in terms of the optimum number of variables used. In a forecasting model, if the inclusion of an additional variable reduces the observed error $(\Sigma y_i - \hat{y}_i)$ by an insignificant amount, then the new variable should be disregarded.

Sometimes little improvement is made after, say, two variables have entered the equation. It can also be shown mathematically that, after a number of variables have been entered, the addition of more variables to an equation will sometimes result in an increase of the standard error of the estimate. The standard error is computed by:

$$Sy.x = \sqrt{\frac{\sum_{t=1}^{n} (y_t - \hat{y}_t)^2}{n - k}}$$

where:

n = number of observations

k = number of variables

Using the basic calculation of the regression, the standard error can be estimated as follows:

$$Sy.x = \sqrt{\frac{\Sigma y^2 - a(\Sigma y) - b\ (\Sigma xy)}{n-k}}$$

Since one degree of freedom is lost for every independent variable added, a point will be reached at which the denominator will begin decreasing at a faster rate than the numerator. Although the coefficient of determination will always increase, its rate of increase will continually decline as variables are added.

The inclusion of too many variables can often lead to a multicollinearity situation. Ragnar Frish did extensive work on correlation and regression analysis and found that in multiple regression, when two explanatory (independent) variables are highly correlated among themselves, the errors of the (b) coefficients will be large and the estimates will be biased. A classic example would be:

Participation in sports activities = f (income and education)

In general, income is correlated to education in a reasonably linear fashion. This relationship is called "multicollinearity". Thus, multicollinearity describes a situation where two highly correlated variables are allowed to enter the same equation. In that case, not only is the effect of each variable on the dependent variable clouded, but the least-squares regression technique tends to break down. Indeed one of the main assumptions of regression analysis is that no two independent variables or no two groups (strictly linear combinations) of independent variables should be identical. If this assumption is violated, estimates of the coefficients of the equation cannot be obtained by least-squares regression analysis because a singular matrix is obtained which cannot be inverted for estimation. Multicollinearity does make parameter estimation unstable since it tends to increase the estimated variance of the estimator. Interrelations among the explanatory variables, if present, can affect the estimates of all the parameters of the relationship since regression analysis cannot completely separate the individual effects of several interrelated explanatory variables. The presence of multicollinearity in a set of observations is often recognized by rules of thumb, such as coefficients with wrong sign or low t-ratios along with a high value of (R^2). It should be emphasized, however, that nearly all socio-economic variables observed over time are intercorrelated and it is only very high degrees of association that cause problems.

When the model is correctly stated but some variables have the incorrect signs, one of the first things to suspect is the existence of multicollinearity. When multicollinearity exists, the "forecasting model" is better off than the "explanatory model". If in the future the multicollinearity is expected to continue at about the same level, then the intercorrelation may not distort the results significantly. Thus, if forecasting is a primary objective, then multicollinearity may not be too serious a problem. In sports and recreation many of the explanatory socio-economic variables are highly correlated such as income, age and education, but these intercorrelations can reasonably be expected to continue in the future. The normal solution to correct for multicollinearity is the rejection of one of the variables. This could be costly for an "explanatory" model, where an estimate of the various coefficients is required. However, in "forecasting models" if one variable will do the work of two, no loss is incurred and the forecast is simplified. The choice of which variable to remove is not easy however, and there is no a priori rules in a retaining one variable or another. Judgement should be used, and be guided by the following considerations:

• The easier variable to forecast should be retained. However, by definition multicollinearity implies similar variability. Only those independent variables which can be forecasted within a reasonable degree of accuracy should be used. Estimating procedure is only as good as the quality of the future estimates of the independent variables. Nevertheless, sometimes official forecasts of only one variable exist and such variables should therefore be retained; and

- The variable to be retained should be the one which has a more logical causality with the dependent variable.

An editing activity should therefore always precede the definition of the model structure to determine on a purely logical basis whether or not a certain variable may affect another in a significant way. Such preliminary investigation may reveal that certain suspected correlations, although qualitatively existent, are quantitatively insignificant in view of the required accuracy and would therefore unnecessarily complicate the model.

4)   **Selecting Too Few Variables**

If significant variables are not included in the model, even though they may be outside the scope of the correlations to be investigated, the model will not be reliable. When conceptually a certain variable should be included in the model, then, even if its contribution in explaining the total variance is small, it should be retained. A model with fewer variables is, of course, easier to handle and requires less work in terms of forecasting the future level of the explanatory variables. However, it also relies on fewer variables, and any error in these variables takes on a greater importance and could seriously affect the quality of the forecasts.

5)   **Signs of Independent Variables**

Logic must be considered when examining the positive or negative contribution of the independent variables. However, in some cases the contribution to the estimate of the dependent variables appears to be illogical when in fact the theory needs to be modified. For example, the author measured sports participation of a sample of University of Ottawa students. The sign of the "income" variable was always negative, which contradicts the normal positive relationship between income and sports participation. However, in the case of students the reverse is true: "the higher the income of students the less his/her available time and therefore his/her participation". As well, particular attention should be given to conflicting facilities like swimming, fishing or boating when they take place in the same recreational site. A multiple-use recreation site may create conflicts and affect participation in an unexpected way.

6)   **Range**

Regression equations are often linear approximations of more complex relationships. This can lead to some serious problems. The most major problem is that outside of the range of the observed statistical relationship, it may not hold. Consider for example the relationship between leisure and income. Over some range more income leads to more leisure, but higher levels of income may eventually restrain free time and negatively affect the pursuit of leisure. Another example is the relationship between the amount of snowfall and the number of skiers at ski resorts. Up to a point, an increase in snowfall will attract more skiers. However, past a certain level, large quantities of snow will reduce attendance at ski resorts.

7)   **Errors of Specification (Es) and Errors of Measurement (Em)**

i)   Error of specification is related to the statistical concept of bias. It arises from the use of a simple model of the real-world situation. The simplest case is perhaps the use of a linear function to represent a non-linear process (Es). A more common and less obvious error of specification is the omission of some key variable or a substitution by another variable due to lack of data. For instance, assume that past research in a cross-sectional model indicates that "household income" is a better variable to use, both statistically and from a conceptual point of view, than personal income. However, if no household income data are available and the forecaster had to use a substitute such as "average per capita income", the quality of the forecast would be affected. Of course it is impossible to ascertain if "household income" would improve the fit on a time-series basis, but the omission of this variable could increase the specification error. In most cases, the forecaster cannot measure the loss due to an omitted variable.

ii)   Measurement error (Em) is related to the statistical concept of "sampling error". It arises from the inaccuracies involved in attempting to measure a magnitude from a limited set of observations. These can be shown graphically in Figure 9.1.

FIGURE 9.1

TYPES OF ERRORS IN FORECASTING

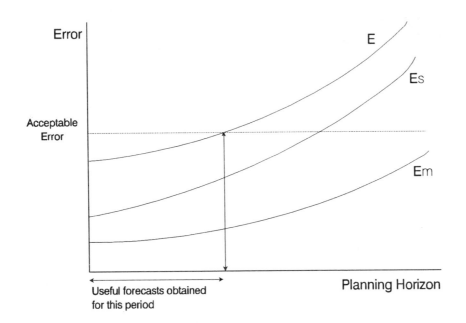

As we extend the forecasting period, specification error may become worse for a variety of reasons. Specification error increases if we attempt to apply a simple representation of a complex situation outside the range of values on which the model was based, or if the structure of the situation changes because of shifts in the underlying economic, social, and behavioral processes. This argument suggests that as the forecasting period increases, more complex models resembling the actual situation more closely, should be used in order to reduce specification error. However, as models become more complex or "more fully specified", measurement error increases and may at some point outweigh these gains. Although this argument lacks mathematical rigour, it appears to suggest some fairly sound guidelines for the selection of models.

8)   **Unforeseeable Changes**

The unforeseeable changes, including technological innovations and political factors, or changes in priorities such as budgetary variations, introduce a high element of uncertainty into the calculation. Figure 9.2 shows the erratic fluctuations in the operating budget of a recreation organization. If participation in recreational activities is affected by the quality of recreation services which in turn are related to the budget, one can see the difficulty in forecasting when recreation budgets are volatile from year to year.

FIGURE 9.2

UNFORESEEABLE CHANGES

FLUCTUATIONS IN OPERATING BUDGET

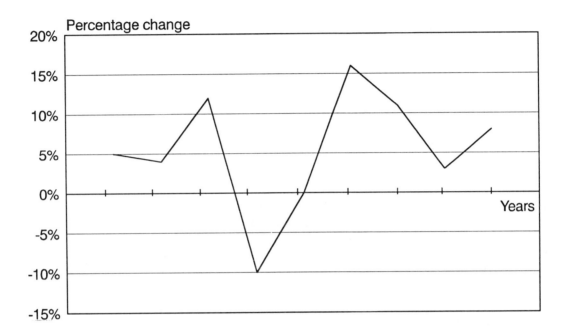

In consequence, it is somewhat unrealistic to expect a high measure of forecast accuracy for more than a few years ahead, and even then the degree of precision is likely to diminish considerably towards the end of the forecast period.

9)   **Special Events**

In the area of sports and recreation, the dependent variables are sometimes affected by exogenous variables which are not necessarily an integral part of the underlying trend. For instance, attendance in specific recreation sites might be positively or negatively affected by a special event (carnival, fair, exhibition, etc...). These events are practically impossible to forecast unless their occurrence is on a continuous basis. Two approaches might be used in treating such exogenous variables:

i)   neglect their impact and treat them as part of the regular time series, hoping that the trend will not be too erratic; and/or.

ii)   subtract their values from the initial trend.

10)   **Outliers**

An outlier is an observation which is "outside" the accepted trend. A single outlier can have a significant impact on the correlation coefficient and can bias the coefficients and undermine the forecasting results. Consider the following scatter diagram:

FIGURE 9.3

SCATTER DIAGRAM

PRESENCE OF OUTLIERS

(outliers are encircled)

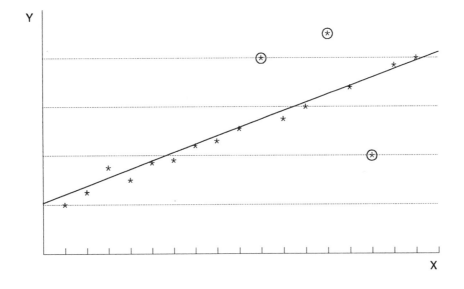

One method to detect outliers is to standardize the residuals (error terms, ε_i), that is divide them by the standard error (S_ε) and then plot them on a graph in relation to the estimated values. Every point distant from ($\bar{\varepsilon}$) = 0 could be an outlier. The errors (ε_i) are supposed to have a normal distribution, and 95% of the values of such a distribution are located within (-2) and (+2). Thus, any point outside the range of the two lines is an outlier, as illustrated in Figure 9.4.

FIGURE 9.4
DISTRIBUTION OF ERRORS

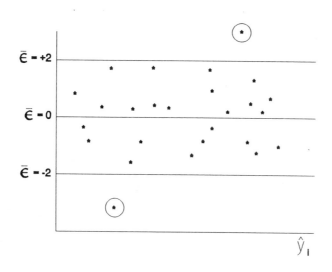

11)   **Saturation**

One aspect that should receive particular attention in connection with any forecast, specifically particular in the area of sports and recreation, is saturation. Too often this is ignored or assumed to be adequately considered when the specific determinants of the quantity demanded (e.g. participants, or sales) are analyzed, such as price or income.

Consider the following forecasting equation:

$$y = a + b_1 x_1 + b_2 x_2 + b_3 x_3$$

where:

y = attendance at a recreation site

x_1 = temperature variations

x_2 = regional population

x_3 = publicity expenditures

If $(x_1, x_2,$ *and* $x_3)$ are positively correlated with (y), then projecting high values of these variables would produce high levels of attendance (y). However, a forecast might be made projecting total attendance at levels which could exceed the capacity of the recreation site. The forecast must therefore devote particular attention to establishing a limit or saturation point. A few remarks should be made about saturation points:

. At any one time there is such a saturation point. However, the point may change through time, for instance if the capacity of the site is augmented; and

. There may be factors existing in the demand situation which are presently constant or dormant but which may become active at some point of time in the future.

Saturation may be also measured from the demand side. If we have 10 million households and they posses 3 million boats, the market may be said to be 30 percent saturated. However if the average boat price is $5,000 and the large majority of boat owners and purchasers earn over $60,000 a year, then we should mainly be concerned with households earning an income of $60,000 a year or more. In this case the saturation ratio may be 75 percent if the number of households in this income group is 4 million.

Thus, even if an equation yields good results and a "back testing" is carried out in a satisfactory manner, saturation variables may invalidate the prediction powers of the equation. Indeed it is quite possible to improve the coefficient of determination (R^2) by manipulating the independent variables until the fit is improved. However, if saturation was not taken into account, the forecasting accuracy of the equation is negatively affected.

12) **Overfitting**

Overfitting occurs when too many independent variables are used to attempt to explain the variation in the dependent variable. It may also arise when there are not enough data points. If the number of independent variables is close to the number of observations, a good fit may be obtained, but the coefficient and variance estimates will be poor.

13) **Statistical Inference**

Statistical inference means making a probability judgement concerning the forecast. Thus statistical inference is the basis for making decisions because it lends a statistical validity to the forecast. This validity is reflected by using specific statistics such as the "F" and the "t" tests. Often a forecaster would concentrate on (R) or (R^2) and neglect other statistical tests which can detect serious problems with the forecasting results.

14) **Forecasting Technique**

Many forecasters select the easiest method or the one for which they have a computer program. The selected technique should suit the type of data, and in some cases, a few trials are needed before deciding upon the final forecasting method.

15)   Subjectivity

While it is recommended to adjust the forecasts subjectively, this approach is acceptable provided the adjustment was the result of sound judgement or the consensus of operational management. When this is not the case, such adjustment would then lead to errors.

9.3 ERRORS

"The problem is not whether you can see the handwriting on the wall, but whether you can read it".

Evan Esar

1)   Sources

The basic regression model always contains an error term which is defined as:

$$\varepsilon_t = y_t - \hat{y}_t$$

where:

ε_t = error

y_t = actual observations

$\hat{y}_t$ = the calculated predicted values

The error term has three sources:

i)   *Specification Error*

Specification errors stem from the fact that the forecaster uses a simple model in a computer situation. In this case the model does not include variables which should have been included. The most common case is when a linear function is applied in a non-linear case. For example:

Attendance at a ski resort = f (snowfall)

While snowfall has an impact on attendance, other variables should also be included in order to reflect the "real world situation", such as:

- miles of trails,
- publicity,
- number of ski instructors,
- etc...

The effect of all these omitted variables is captured by the error term. The omission of some key explanatory variables would increase the error term, affect the forecast and yield a lower correlation coefficient.

ii)   *Measurement Error*

Sports and recreation data are not always easy to measure with complete accuracy. Measurement errors are due to:

- recording,
- rounding,
- estimation,

- missing data,

- etc...

Thus the errors are due to the underlying theoretical model and are not related to the regression line. A visual presentation of the errors is shown in Figure 9.5.

FIGURE 9.5
VISUAL PRESENTATION OF ERROR TERMS

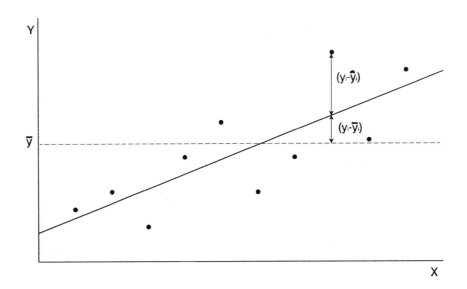

A few observations can be made about the above figure:

- In the absence of a regression line, the mean $(\bar{y})$ can be used to relate the observed to the average. If we forecast by using the average, the error would be large $(Y_i - \bar{Y})$;

- Using regression analysis would reduce the error. Indeed,

$$\hat{Y}_i - \bar{Y} < Y_i - \bar{Y} \quad ;$$

. Total deviation can be looked at as the sum of two errors:

$$Y_i - \bar{Y} = \text{total deviation,}$$

$$\hat{Y}_i - \bar{Y} = \text{deviation explained by regression,}$$

$$Y_i - \hat{Y} = \text{deviation not explained by regression, so that:}$$

$$(Y_i - \bar{Y}) = (\hat{Y}_i - \bar{y}) + (y_i - \hat{y}_i);$$

- The above equation also holds when the deviations are squared:

$$\Sigma (Y_i - \bar{Y})^2 = \Sigma (\hat{Y}_i - \bar{y})^2 + \Sigma (y_i - \hat{y}_i)^2;$$

- It is also convenient to express the errors in terms of (x) :

$$\Sigma (Y_i - \bar{Y})^2 = b_1 \Sigma (x_i - \bar{x})^2 + \Sigma (y_i - \hat{y}_i)^2$$

Total variation = variation explained by (x) + unexplained variation.

It is interesting to note that the coefficient of determination (R^2) can be expressed as the ratio between the "explained variation" and "total variation":

$$R^2 = \frac{\sum (\hat{y}_i - \bar{y})^2}{\sum (y_i - \bar{y})^2}$$

iii)   ***Sampling Error***

The errors can be also related to the sample used to estimate the forecasting model. If the sample does not reflect the characteristics of the population, the results would be biased and inaccurate forecasts would be obtained.

2)   **Type**

When the forecasting technique does not fit the data trend, the error terms would reflect a systematic pattern. A basic condition of regression analysis is that the errors are randomly distributed with a zero mean. This is illustrated in Figure 9.6:

FIGURE 9.6

RANDOM DISTRIBUTION OF ERRORS

ZERO MEAN

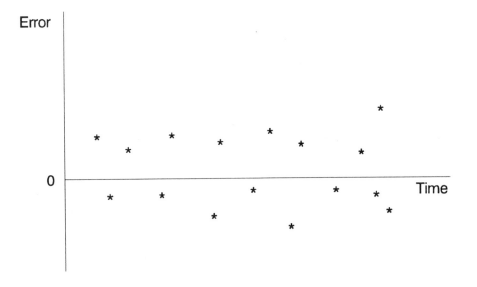

Sometimes this is not the case. Errors might have an upward linear trend or a cyclical trend:

FIGURE 9.7

UPWARD TREND IN ERRORS

FIGURE 9.8

CYCLICAL TREND IN ERRORS

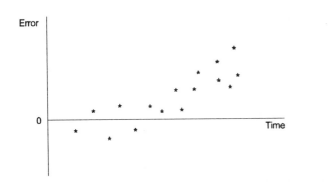

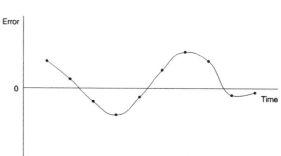

or a seasonal pattern:

FIGURE 9.9

SEASONAL PATTERN IN ERRORS

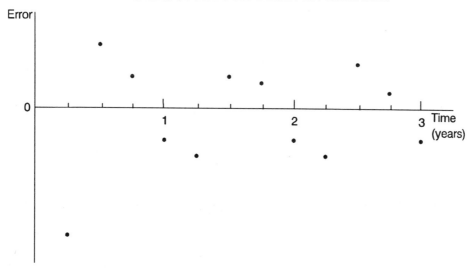

While the visual presentation of the error terms serves a useful function, it cannot by itself be a fool-proof technique to identify the type of errors mainly due to the following:

- sometimes the scatter diagram of the errors exhibits no discernible pattern;
- it is difficult to compare the merits of alternative forecasting methods just by using a graphical aid; and
- the forecaster will not know if the model has missed some systematic pattern until after the fact.

3)   Evaluation

The level of (R) or (R^2) and the statistical significance of the regression coefficients are reasonable statistics to assess a forecasting method. However, the direct approach to evaluate the forecasting error $(y_i - \hat{y}_i)$ is probably the best method of assessment. This can be done by applying the "accuracy index" which is the degree to which the predicted values, or $(\hat{y}_i)$, diverges from the actual (y_i) for each observation can be easily calculated. The difference between these two is the residual in the regression equation (Residual = Data - Fit). Hence we might use as an index of the accuracy of the forecast the following ratio:

$$\frac{\sum_{i=1}^{n} (y_i - \hat{y}_i)^2}{\sum_{i=1}^{n} (y_i - \bar{y})^2}$$

which can be interpreted as the degree to which efforts of prediction of (y_i) given the set of $(x_i's)$ are smaller than efforts of prediction given no information about the $(x_i's)$. The lower limit of this ratio is zero (numerator is zero). In this case, given the $(x_i's)$ the prediction of (y_i) is perfect. The upper limit of the ratio is one $(\hat{y}_i = \bar{y})$ 33, in which case we have gained no predictive power from the set of $(x_i's)$ at all. Using data from Table 9.1, we obtain 0.54.

9.4 CHECKING THE ACCURACY OF THE FORECAST

"We should take great care how general propositions escape us".

Voltaire

Once a forecast has been made, the following question arises: "How good is the forecast?" The question might be stated: "Over the forecast period, how close is the correspondence between the forecasted values and the actual values?" It is therefore essential to measure the accuracy of the forecast. Although accuracy is an important factor in selecting a forecasting method, it is difficult to agree on a single universally accepted measure of accuracy. The following measures are more relevant for forecasting purposes:

1)   **Past Forecasts**

No matter how careful the forecaster is in selecting and applying a specific forecasting method, the bottom line is its accuracy. If the method has been used in the past and there exists past forecast values and past actual values of the data to be forecasted, it is relatively easy to evaluate the accuracy of the method. However, even then, past performance might not be a guaranty for present or future performance, in particular when past forecasts were made several years ago. For instance, consider the following model:

$$y = f(x)$$

where:

y = change in the number of tourists travelling from country A to country B.

x = the exchange rate between the two countries.

If this model is used over a certain period where the exchange rate was highly in favour of country A, a reliable forecast might be established on the basis of the exchange rate. However, when the exchange rate is neutral, the exchange rate would cease to be an essential forecasting variable and other variables would have more importance. Thus, forecasting models which previously yielded good results may cease to be valid if the forecasted environment has been subject to serious modifications.

2)   **Simulation of Past**

If past forecast data does not exist, the model can be estimated using only past data that would have been available to the forecaster at the time the forecast would have been made. For example, if the forecaster is attempting to forecast enrolment in sports activities for year 16 using the level of household income, then the model should be estimated using past data over the period, say, year 1 to year 13. The resulting equation would then be used to forecast year 14 and year 15, two years for which actual enrolment data exist. This approach would give some idea how well the forecast method could be expected to do. The following example using Table 9.1 illustrates this method:

TABLE 9.1
ACTUAL AND PREDICTED NUMBER OF ENROLMENTS

Year	Actual Enrolment	Estimated Enrolment
1	200	207
2	210	214
3	225	221
4	230	227
5	239	234
6	250	241
7	242	248
8	259	255
9	265	261
10	254	268
11	272	275
12	285	282
13	290	289
14	299	*295*
15	312	*302*

The estimated equation $Y = -13,226 + 6.7912(year)$ yields estimated enrolments of 295 (for year 14) and 302 (for year 15) as opposed to actual enrolments of 299 and 312 for the same respective years.

3)   **Benchmark Forecasts**

Forecasters can initially use simple naïve or numerical methods to get benchmark forecasts on which to base some idea of how well their forecasts can be expected to perform. Thus, if these simple forecasts are able to perform as well, or nearly as well as a more complex forecast, then the forecaster should reconsider the usage of complicated forecast methods.

4)   **Error Approach**

The difference between the actual data (Y) and the forecasted data (Ŷ) is the error term. Thus:

$$Y = \hat{y} + \varepsilon$$

Error values could be used to evaluate the performance of the model. To illustrate the use of errors, examine past forecasts of the number of skaters over 16 previous winter weekends in Winterville.

<u>TABLE 9.2</u>

**ACTUAL AND PREDICTED NUMBER OF SKATERS
WINTER WEEKENDS IN WINTERVILLE**

<u>Weekend</u>	<u>Actual</u>	<u>Predicted</u>	<u>Error</u>
1	2,650	2,726	-76
2	2,790	2,804	-14
3	3,200	2,881	319
4	3,800	2,958	842
5	2,800	3,053	-235
6	2,400	3,113	-713
7	3,000	3,190	-190
8	3,200	3,267	-67
9	3,400	3,344	56
10	3,700	3,422	279
11	3,300	3,499	-199
12	3,400	3,576	-176
13	3,500	3,653	-153
14	3,250	3,731	-481
15	3,900	3,808	92
16	4,600	3,885	715

The average error is a quantifiable and useful statistic in evaluating the performance of the forecasting model. It is defined as:

$$\bar{\varepsilon} = \frac{\sum\limits_{i=1}^{N} (y_i - \hat{y}_i)}{N}$$

where:

y_i = the actual values of the dependent variable (the variable to be predicted).

$\hat{y}_i$ = the predicted values.

N = number of observations.

Because positive and negative errors do cancel each other out, the signs should be ignored when adding up the errors. Applying this measure to the errors calculated in Table 9.2 we obtain:

$$\bar{\varepsilon} = \frac{346.2}{16} = 21.6$$

An average often masks wide variations. Consider for instance two models which give rise to about the same "average error". However, one model may have "several" small errors while the other may produce "a few" large errors. In forecasting it is generally accepted that the cost of an error in the forecast rises proportionally with the size of the error. Relying on the arithmetic average does not penalize for models which have highly unacceptable errors. For this reason the mean square error is more acceptable.

Sometimes, the value of the errors can be expressed as a percentage of the actual number of skaters, e.g., 76 as a percentage of 2,650 = 2.9%. Using data from Table 9.2, we obtain the data as shown in Table 9.3.

TABLE 9.3

ERRORS EXPRESSED AS A PERCENTAGE OF ACTUAL OBSERVATIONS

Weekend	Error (Absolute Value)	Errors as a Percentage of Actual
1	76	2,9
2	14	0,5
3	319	10,0
4	842	22,2
5	235	8,4
6	713	29,7
7	190	6,3
8	67	2,1
9	56	1,6
10	279	7,5
11	199	6,0
12	176	5,2
13	153	4,4
14	481	14,8
15	92	2,4
16	715	15,5

The average prediction error of the forecasting model is = 8.7%

$$\frac{\Sigma \; errors \; as \; a \; percentage \; of \; actual \; observations}{Number \; of \; observations}$$

$$= \frac{139.5}{16}$$

$$= 8.7 \; percent$$

Like any other average it hides wide fluctuations, from a low of 0.5% to a high of 29.7%. Is this performance acceptable to the forecaster? Can the forecaster take specific actions, such as hiring personnel or budget predictions, based on this model? There are no set rules on limits for accepting or rejecting a model. It all depends on the degree of tolerance of the forecaster and the purpose of the model. In general, if the forecaster is not satisfied with the size of the prediction error, he should first try to "re-specify" the form of the model (e.g., non-linear, or logarithmic) or introduce a new explanatory variable.

5)   **Graphical Analysis**

i) Errors

One method of determining the reliability of a forecasting technique is a simple graphical inspection of the error terms. If a particular method forecasts accurately, the error should be randomly distributed, as illustrated in Figure 9.6.

ii) Actual and Predicted Values

The use of graphs is a simple and effective method of forecast evaluation. Actual and predicted values are plotted as in Figure 9.10.

FIGURE 9.10
ACTUAL AND PREDICTED VALUES OF NUMBER OF SKATERS

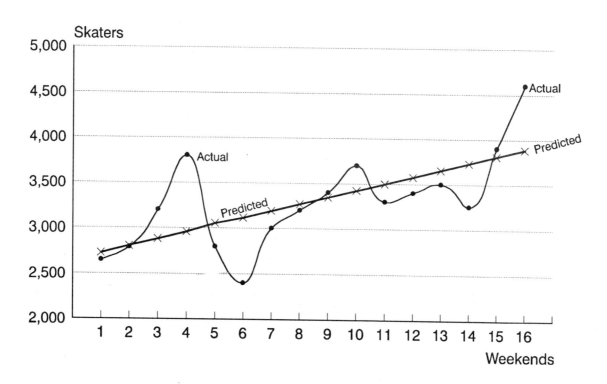

The graph clearly shows periods of "overprediction" and "underprediction". The rate of change in the variable is also a powerful tool to evaluate the forecasting method. Concentrating on the weekly change in the number of skaters can provide a more accurate evaluation method. The following figure shows the actual and the predicted change.

FIGURE 9.11

CHANGE IN ACTUAL AND PREDICTED VALUES

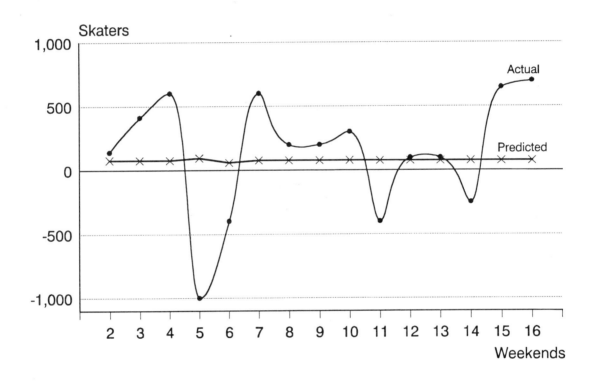

The forecast shows that when the rates of change are low the model overpredicts and underpredicts when the rates of change are high. Thus, a criterion of forecast accuracy is the absence of systematic patterns in the distribution of forecast errors. The forecast errors may be positive in some periods and negative in others, but, over time, their sum should approach zero. If this is true, then we should be able to improve upon our results by adjusting the forecast for this persistent tendency to underestimate or overestimate actual changes. The non-zero sum of forecast errors results either from the choice of an inappropriate model to represent the systematic variations in the variables or as the result of shifts in the way certain variables are related. In either case, a persistent non-zero sum of errors should be a warning to the forecaster that his/her model is no longer providing an adequate representation of reality. Such a warning is easily obtained in practice through use of the graphic device of the Control Chart as illustrated Figure 9.12:

FIGURE 9.12
ERRORS CONTROL CHART

The standard error is calculated using the formula $\sqrt{\dfrac{1}{T} \sum\limits_{t=1}^{T} (\varepsilon_t - \bar{\varepsilon})^2}$ where $(\bar{\varepsilon})$ is the average of forecast errors up to time period (T). In this example, the cumulative sum of forecast errors is always negative. The data suggest that the underlying model has a persistent tendency to underestimate (Y). We can control limits. If it falls within the limits, one can interpret the results as having arisen by chance. If it goes out of control, there is something wrong. We then search for the cause of the problem. Sometimes, no matter how extensive the search, the forecaster will be unable to locate the source of the difficulty.

6)   **Theil's Inequality Coefficient**

Theil's inequality coefficient is defined as:

$$U = \frac{\sqrt{\frac{1}{n}\sum (F_i - A_i)^2}}{\sqrt{\frac{1}{n}\sum F_i^2} + \sqrt{\frac{1}{n}\sum A_i^2}}$$

where:

F_i = forecasted values of a time series

A_i = actual values of the time series.

It should be obvious that it is the numerator that is most important. It measures the actual forecast error obtained. The denominator merely gives us a base measure against which we can compare our results. If the predicted and actual values are identical, then the numerator of (U) will be zero. Thus, a perfect forecast is obtained when (U = 0). At the other extreme, (U = 1) would be a case of all incorrect forecasts. This statistic can be used:

i)   to compare the forecast being evaluated by one forecasting method versus another; and

ii)   to compare the forecast against the actual level of the variable forecasted, or, the change observed may be compared with the change forecasted.

One of the useful features of Theil's Inequality Coefficient is that it is a pure number, unaffected by the size of the units being forecasted. Thus it makes no difference whether, for example, forecasts are in dollars or in number of participants. The Theil coefficients of any two sets of forecasts are always comparable. Sometimes the square of (U) is used (U^2), where ($U^2=1$) would then be the dividing line. ($U^2<1$) indicates that the forecasts are better than those which would have been obtained using, say, a naïve method. A value of ($U^2>1$) indicates the opposite. For a perfect forecast ($U^2=0$). Note that there is no upper limit on the value of (U^2), which simply indicates that there is no limit to how bad you can do.

9.5 IMPROVING THE FORECASTS

"Having accurate forecasts might leave us about as badly off as we were without them. For now we are in the position of having to forecast what those with forecasts will do".

Maurice W. Lee

Forecasts are not fixed in time. A model developed fifteen years ago to forecast the number of skiers may include variables such as equipment for artificial snow-making and slope grooming. Today these variables may have less relevance, and new variables need to be introduced to reflect the current demand. Thus constant monitoring and adjustment are required to ensure that the variables used in the past are still effective and have forecasting power.

In general, the following guidelines can be used to improve the forecast:

1)   State the forecasting problem in a clear way.

2)   Many forecasting techniques are available. Choose the most adequate technique for your situation and your data.

3)   Do not try to fit the situation to a forecast. Instead, fit a forecasting method to a situation.

4) Avoid "gold-plating". If a simple technique or just common sense can be used, why apply complex methods? Thus, a simple forecasting technique should be tried first, before considering a complex one.

5) Make sure you understand the forecasting technique before using it.

6) Adjust the forecasts when conditions change.

7) Evaluate the forecasting method by conforming the actual results with the forecast.

8) Update your data regularly.

9) Evaluate your theoretical model to ensure that important variables were not left out.

10) Use methods which can easily be understood by the decision-makers.

While the above suggestions surely improve our forecast, a few assents should always be in our mind when we deliver a forecast, namely:

. Some situations can be forecasted with a common-sense rule. In that case, avoid using statistical techniques.

. The future is probabilistic and there is no way to have a perfect vision of things to come.

. The forecast will work as long as the established patterns do not change. Errors will occur if pattern changes and the errors do not have to follow the established pattern. The errors could be random, and, therefore beyond the forecasted pattern.

- Forecasting is only one step in the whole planning process and it should not be considered as the sole basis for decision-making.

- The methods used, no matter how sophisticated they are, should always be supplemented by judgement. This fact is often neglected, and forecasters work diligently to substitute judgement by empirical evidence and complex methods.

- Key events are often omitted from the forecast. This will occur for several reasons, such as lack of information or simply introduction of outside disturbances.

- The interpretation of a forecast. Often a forecast is interpreted as a level which will be attained with high probability. If the actual performance is different from the expected performance, the forecaster will tend to review his tools in order to improve the forecast. However, a forecast always contains a set of assumptions, the most obvious being that management will continue to manage at least at the same level of efficiency as in the past. Any deviation from this implicit assumption will invalidate the forecast.

9.6 STUDY QUESTIONS

1) Is there a trade-off between the "accuracy" of a forecast and the "costs" of preparing the forecast? Explain.

2) Why is "simplicity" a desirable feature of a forecasting model?

3)   "A wise forecaster should not select independent variables which are difficult to forecast even if they yield good forecasting results". Why? Provide an example to support your answer.

4)   Why does "linearity" lead to serious problems in the forecasting range?

5)   How can you reduce the risk of "errors of measurement"?

6)   Provide an example of:

-    Unforeseeable changes in forecasting the results of a swimming contest.
-    Unforeseeable changes in predicting enrolment in the school of physical education.

7)   How can "special events" be treated in a forecasting exercise?

8)   Should we reject "outliers"? What can they reveal?

9)   What are the main sources of "mesurement errors"? Provide an example.

10)   What will be the effect of omitting some key independent variables from a forecasting model?

9.7 BIBLIOGRAPHY

ADELSON, M.
1985   "Bringing The Future Down to Earth", *Futures Research Quarterly*, Vol. 1, 63-73.

ASCHER, W.
1978   *Forecasting: An Appraisal for Policy-Makers and Planners*, Baltimore: The Johns Hopkins University Press.

ASKIN, R.S.
1982   "Multicollinearity in Regression: Review and Examples", *Journal of Forecasting*, Vol. 1, 281-292.

BEAMAN, J.
1982   Comments on an Article: The Relative Performance of Various Estimators of Recreation Participation Equations", *Journal of Leisure Research*, Vol. 14, 266-272.

BELSLEY, D.A.
1984   "Collinearity and Forecasting", *Journal of Forecasting*, Vol. 3, 183-196.

BULL, C.N.
1972   "Prediction of Future Daily Behaviors: An Empirical Measure of Leisure", *Journal of Leisure Research*, Vol. 4, 119-128.

EINHORN, H.J. and R.M. HOGARTH
1982   "Prediction, Diagnosis, and Causal Thinking in Forecasting", *Journal of Forecasting*, Vol. 1 (1), 23-36.

ELSNER, G.H.
1971   "Using Error Measures to Compare Models on Recreation Use", *Journal of Leisure Research*, Vol. 3, 277-280.

GODET, M.
1991   "From Anticipation to Action", *Futuribles*, Vol. 156, 31-38.

GRANGER, C.W. and R. RAMANATHAN
1984   "Improved Methods of Combining Forecasts", *Journal of Forecasting*, Vol.3, 197-204.

HEDLEY, R.W. and D. MORIARTY
1980   *Evaluation and Forecast of Future Directions of the Ontario Federation of School Athletic Associations*, Arlington, VA: ERIC.

HILLMER, S.
1984 "Monitoring and Adjusting Forecasts in the Presence of Additive Outliers", *Journal of Forecasting*, Vol. 3, 205-215.

LAPLANTE, M.J. and A.E. JEWETT
1987 Content Validation of the Purpose Dimension, *Journal of Teaching in Physical Education*, 6 (3), 214-223.

LITTLE, C.H.
1986 "Who Forecasts Better - Business People or Professional Forecasters?", *Futures Research Quarterly*, Vol. 2, 39-52.

MAHMOUD, E.
1984 "Accuracy in Forecasting: A Survey", *Journal of Forecasting*, Vol. 3, 139-159.

MENTZER, J.T. and J.E. COX, Jr.
1984 "Familiarity, Application, and Performance of Sales Forecasting Techniques", *Journal of Forecasting*, Vol. 3, 27-36.

MOELLER, G.H. and H.E. ECHELBERGER
1974 Approaches to Forecasting Recreation Consumption, *Outdoor Recreation Research: Applying the Results*, Technical Report NC-9, North Central Forest Experimental Station, St. Paul, Minn: Forest Service, U.S. Dept. of Agriculture.

NG, D.
1988 Forecasting Leisure Futures: Methodological Issues, *Recreation Research Review*, 13 (4), 32-38.

SCHULKE, H.J.
1980 Changes in Sport Habits and Their Significance for the Forecasting of Future Forms of Physical Culture, *International Review of Sport Sociology*, 15, 3-4, 105-121.

SHELDON, P.J. and T. VAR
1985 "Tourism Forecasting: A Review of Empirical Research, *Journal of Forecasting*, Vol. 4, 183-196.

STRZEMINSKA, H.
1973 "Use of Time-Budgets Data for Diagnosis and Prognosis: Some Remarks on the Practical Application of Results of Time-Budget Investigation", *Society and Leisure*, Vol. 5 (1), 49-69.

TSAY, R.S.
1988 "Outliers, Level Shifts, and Variance Changes in Time Series", *Journal of Forecasting*, Vol. 7, 1-20.

VEAL, A.J.
1992 *Research Methods for Leisure and Tourism: A Practical Guide.*

VEAL, A.J.
1980 *Trends in Leisure Participation and Problems in Forecasting: The State of the Art*, A Report to the Sports Council/SSRC Panel on Leisure Research, London: Sports Council.

WALSH, R.G.
1986 *Recreation Economic Decisions: Comparing Benefits and Costs*, State College, Pennsylvania: Venture Publishing, Inc.

WHISTON, T.
1979 *The Uses and Abuses of Forecasting*, London: MacMillan.

WILSON, K.D.
1978 "Forecasting Futures", *Society*, Vol. 15 (2), 22-27.

INDEX